Blessed Is the Man

A Man's Journey through the Psalms

Psalms of Praise

Praise the LORD!
Blessed is the man
who fears the LORD,
who greatly delights
in His commandments!
Psalm 112:1

By Joel D. Biermann, Tim Radkey, Joe Hanson, Michael Zpevak, Mike Furrey, Joshua Salzberg, Fred Gaede, and Jeff Williams

Edited by Robert C. Baker

Unless otherwise indicated, Scripture quotations are from the ESV Bible® (The Holy Bible, English Standard Version®), copyright © 2001 by Crossway Bibles, a publishing ministry of Good News Publishers. Used by permission. All rights reserved.

Hymn texts with the abbreviation *LSB* are from *Lutheran Service Book*, copyright © 2006 Concordia Publishing House. All rights reserved.

Quotations from *Reading the Psalms with Luther*, copyright © 2007 Concordia Publishing House. All rights reserved.

The definition of *Sacrament* on page 234 is adapted from *Luther's Small Catechism with Explanation*, copyright © 1986, 1991 Concordia Publishing House, pp. 202–203.

This publication may be available in braille, in large print, or on cassette tape for the visually impaired. Please allow 8 to 12 weeks for delivery. Write to Lutheran Blind Mission, 7550 Watson Rd., St. Louis, MO 63119-4409; call toll free 1-888-215-2455; or visit the Web site: www.blindmission.org.

1 2 3 4 5 6 7 8 9 10   19 18 17 16 15 14 13 12 11 10

Contents

Meet Our Authors

Joel D. Biermann

Joel resides in St. Louis, Missouri, with his bride of twenty-four years, Jeannalee. Their two daughters, Jasmine and Justine, are Lutheran school teachers, and their son, Jess, is enjoying his formative high school years. Joel's vocation finds him at Concordia Seminary, St. Louis, teaching systematic theology. Leading the list of favorite pastimes is any active outdoor pursuit with Jeannalee, who excels at providing what is best for Joel and their family.

Tim Radkey

Tim, his wife, Lea Ann, and their daughter, Claire, reside in Lubbock, Texas, where Tim serves as lead pastor of Hope Lutheran Church. On weekends, Tim and his family enjoy spending time in the mountains of New Mexico. Tim also runs marathons, rides bicycles, and rides around town on his Harley-Davidson. Tim blogs about his up-and-coming book from CPH at timradkey.wordpress.com.

Joe Hanson

Joe grew up in Asia as a missionary kid, returned while in the U.S. Navy, and lived in Hong Kong while working for a large U.S. corporation. He has a Ph.D. in chemistry. Now retired, Joe and his wife reside in Wheaton, Illinois. They have two grown children. Joe works as an executive coach and an Asia business consultant. Running, including occasional marathons, keeps him active outdoors year-round.

Michael Zpevak

Michael practiced law for over 30 years, including before the United States Supreme Court. For most of his career he was a leading federal regulatory attorney for a large telecommunications firm. A published legal author, Michael has also written a novel and a great deal of music. Now largely retired, Michael plays and runs a ten-piece Classic Rock band, "Nonstop." You can visit the band's Web site at nonstoprock.net.

Mike Furrey

An Ohio native, Mike was a walk-on for the Ohio State Buckeyes. Completing his college career at Northern Iowa, Mike now plays wide receiver for the Cleveland Browns. Mike, his wife, Koren, and children Makayla, Stone Jett, and Kanon reside in Michigan and Ohio where they run the Mike Furrey Foundation. You can learn more about the Furreys' charitable work by logging on to mikefurrey.net.

Joshua Salzberg

Josh was a video manager for the 2007 Lutheran Church—Missouri Synod Youth Gathering and is a regular contributor to LCMS youth ministry publications. He works as a freelance film editor in Los Angeles, California. His wife, Sarah, is a theology teacher at Lutheran High School, Orange County.

Fred Gaede

Fred is the Chief Creative Officer of Boomm Marketing and Communications. His wife, Valerie, is the Director of Preschool for St. John Lutheran Church and School in Wheaton, Illinois. He is the proud father of two sons, John and Matthew. Fred enjoys camping, canoeing and bad movies (unless they star Nicholas Cage, Bruce Willis or Kevin Costner, then he will refuse to watch them), and tries to find time to draw, paint, or play mandolin, banjo, or guitar.

Jeff Williams

Jeff grew up on a farm in the rural community of Winter, Wisconsin. A graduate of West Point, he retired as a colonel in the U.S. Army after twenty-seven years of service. As an astronaut, Jeff flew on the 10-day space shuttle mission STS-101 in 2000 before beginning training for the 183-day Expedition 13 in 2006. Jeff and his wife, Anna-Marie, are members of Gloria Dei Lutheran Church in Houston, Texas. They have two grown sons.

How to Use This Book

This isn't your father's devotional.

Then again, while your father may not have read the stories found in *Blessed Is the Man*, he may have heard stories similar to them. Stories told by his father or brother or friend, real stories from real men who experienced real life relying on God's real—and amazing—grace. Stories like the ones you've heard other believers tell you, or stories you've told yourself.

Blessed Is the Man provides you and your Bible study group with six weeks of faith narratives written by men who have prayerfully considered biblical psalms. At the beginning of each week, you will read an assigned psalm. Five days during that week, you'll read a verse or two of that psalm, followed by the author's story. Next, you may pray a suggested prayer or choose another as you see fit. Finally, you'll answer a few brief Bible study questions that will help you consider other ways the psalm may apply to you. To get the most out of *Blessed Is the Man*, prayerfully review the psalm from time to time throughout the week. Through God's Word, the Holy Spirit will confront and challenge, but He will also comfort and console. At the end of each week, join your brothers in Christ in a group Bible study. Weekly small-group questions are reproducible. If you want to hold your group Bible study before hammering the first nail at a Habitat for Humanity project, at halftime during a televised game, or before you throw the brats on the grill, do so! You may make as many copies of these pages as you need for the guys in your group.

We are grateful that you are taking a man's journey through the Psalms in *Blessed Is the Man*. Along the way, you may be reminded of stories of faith told by your father, brother, or friend. The adventure into God's Word may even inspire you to tell a few of your own.

—The Editor

Suggestions for Small-Group Participants

1. Before you begin, spend some time in prayer, asking God to strengthen your faith through a study of His Word. The Scriptures were written so that we might believe in Jesus Christ and have life in His name (John 20:31).

2. Take some time before the meeting to look over the session, review the psalm, and answer the questions.

3. As a courtesy to others, arrive on time.

4. Be an active participant. The leader will guide the group's discussion, not give a lecture.

5. Avoid dominating the conversation by answering every question or by giving unnecessarily long answers. On the other hand, avoid the temptation to not share at all.

6. Treat anything shared in your group as confidential until you have asked for and received permission to share it outside of the group. Treat information about others outside of your group as confidential until you have asked for and received permission to share it with group members.

7. Some participants may be new to Bible study or new to the Christian faith. Help them feel welcome and comfortable.

8. Affirm other participants when you can. If someone offers what you perceive to be a "wrong" answer, ask the Holy Spirit to guide him to seek the correct answer from God's Word.

9. Keep in mind that the questions are discussion starters. Don't be afraid to ask additional questions that relate to the topic. Don't get the group off track.

10. If you are comfortable doing so, volunteer now and then to pray at the beginning or end of the session.

Guide to Men's Ministry

There's a mother watching her boys play in the backyard. The boys are wrestling around in the mud, fighting to see who will be at the top of the pecking order, as brothers often do. There's another mother in the same backyard who has a little girl, or you might even say a *princess*. She comments, "Don't you think those boys are going to hurt one another? How are you going to get the stains out of their clothes?" To this, the mother of the boys replies, "Boys will be boys." In this short story, it is clear that one mother understands boys and the other has no clue how boys become men.

The sad news is this: the Church in many ways has adopted the voice of the princess's mother who never raised boys. It seems men are expected to live, act, and behave in ways that make sure any remnant of their childhood has been extinguished. Men are tamed to fit the mold of what a good little boy should look like—free of danger, free of risk, and free of anything fun.

Giving men permission to be men once again is absolutely critical to the Church and to a successful men's ministry. There is enough boy left in every man that beckons to compete, have fun, risk, and live out the adventurous spirit only God can give. Yes, it is possible for all of this to happen in the Church while men still live within the will and call of God upon their lives.

Seven Tips for Men's Ministry

GET "REAL" LEADERS

Men desperately need leaders who are authentic, genuine, and nonjudgmental. You must choose a leader whom other men would want to hang out with and can relate to on multiple levels. This is a guy whom other guys love to hang out with because he seems so down to earth, has fun living life, and would be a leader in any environment he found himself in.

THERA-PUKE-IC

Guys need to be in an environment that is natural, not clinical. Guys will share their struggles, challenges, and victories as long as it's not the purpose of the meeting or even the hidden agenda for their time together. When they catch wind that this is about to turn into group therapy, most guys will immediately button their lips, turn off their brains, and look for the nearest exit. When the environment is right, guys will talk. Don't force it. Please, don't force it.

LESS IS MORE

Women are always amazed at how simple men can be at times. Most men like simplicity and are drawn to it. Whether you're planning a men's social, Bible study, retreat, or small group, it is always better to err on the side of keeping it simple. Simple doesn't mean plain or boring; it means doing a few things really, really well. When you sit down to plan activities, try structuring them around broader themes such as having fun, learning a little, and providing a good challenge or risk for men to participate in.

TALKING IS OPTIONAL

Generally when men come together for activities, Bible studies, small groups, and/or retreats, there is going to be a time for prayer, reading, and answering some questions. There are many men who don't like to read out loud, pray out loud, or be put on the spot to answer questions out loud. Be sure to check with guys ahead of time about praying or reading. There will always be a few men who are comfortable answering questions, and these men usually pave the way for more timid guys to speak up.

KEEP THE SPIRIT OF COMPETITION ALIVE

Not all men played sports, but most men have competed as boys in some area or another. Men, by and large, enjoy competition and friendly wagers. Some men like playing golf against one another, while others enjoy seeing who smokes the best brisket. Either way you slice it, men always enjoy themselves when they can compete in a nonthreatening way, in a way that will never leave them feeling foolish in front of one another.

MEETINGS SHOULD NEVER BE MEETINGS

From time to time, there will be a need to plan various activities for men. The worst thing you can do is form a committee or a board. There will always be natural leaders who will need to do some planning for men's ministry, but have the meeting at a place men enjoy, like an athletic event, a pub, or even on a golf course while playing a round. No one, especially men, needs to add more "official" meetings to his schedule. Make it informal and fun while you orchestrate real business.

A MINISTRY NEEDS MORE THAN ONE DOOR

How accessible is your ministry? The fastest-growing churches always have multiple entry points for folks to get involved and be connected to their church. Men's ministry is no different. While there is a tremendous brotherhood among men, there are also a wide range of things that men like and don't like. Some men like camping and the great outdoors. Other men would prefer manual labor around the church. Some might even like more intellectually oriented activities. No matter what, you need to ensure that your men's ministry has many different attractions that respect different interests, gifts, abilities, and skills. There are venues for all men to come together, and there are activities that will only attract certain men. Keep all these nuances in mind.

Three Steps to Launching a Men's Ministry in *Your* Church

LOCATION, LOCATION, LOCATION

Pick a place that will work for launching your first men's ministry event. A tailgate setting would be an absolutely prime site. Other options are at a lake, the rustic outdoors, or even a barn of sorts. Whatever you choose as your site, it should be a place where guys can get excited and loud and not feel closed in.

MEN EAT MEAT AND LOTS OF IT

Once you've got the location nailed down, it's time to think about the meat you are going to serve. Depending on what area of the country you live in, your choices and preferences will vary. One example is having a spread of wild-game dishes. This usually takes place in areas where men enjoy hunting. If you have chosen a tailgate at some sporting event, cook up a bunch of bratwurst, brisket, and/or ribs. Warning: it's tough to cook a great steak when you're doing it in large numbers. Men are picky with their steaks, so be careful if this is your choice. Don't forget to bring beverages that your men would enjoy as well. (Okay, you can throw on some veggie burgers too.)

IT'S TIME TO LAUNCH—THE DAY IS HERE

Okay, you've chosen a great site. You've got the volunteers you need to cook the meat at the site. Now it's time to plan how you are going to effectively brainstorm what your men's ministry might look like. This is not a time to be critical of ideas. This is a time to really listen to what men are saying.

What kinds of activities do they want to be involved with?

What kinds of adventures are they looking for?

What contribution do they want their men's ministry to make to the kingdom of God externally and to their church internally?

Make this fun. For example, to get things started, you could have some balloons attached to a big piece of plywood and have various ideas written on slips of paper inside the balloons. Have one of the men use the BB gun you provided to shoot one of the balloons and see what idea is inside and talk about it. This exercise can be a lot of fun, but please be safe with it. Once you have some good ideas about the direction the men would like to go, pick another time and location to meet again and flesh out more of the details and planning. Ask for any volunteers who want to help with this next phase. Once this next phase is finished, you should be able to get to work—but don't forget to keep on listening to the men in your church.

Introduction

It was the standard Sunday morning routine when I was a growing up. Arriving at church early—even earlier when there was fresh snow that had to be shoveled off the long stretches of concrete sidewalk—my two younger brothers and I would wait for 9:00 with all the enthusiasm of a man anticipating the first light of dawn and, with it, a place before the firing squad. Delaying the inevitable well past what might be deemed acceptable, we would finally shuffle in at the last possible moment and take our spots in the front pews of the church—left side. And then she would appear. Sometimes from behind the organ, where she had been looking over the morning's hymns or the choir's number (always a well-worn favorite of somebody's that hadn't been heard for as long as a full year), sometimes coming down the center aisle, coffee in hand (even later than we had hoped to be), she would make her entrance. Then, with arms flailing wildly but purposefully, and with faultless, eternal enthusiasm, Mrs. G. would direct the gathered Sunday School students in the first obligatory "praise chorus" that marked the official beginning of another Sunday morning of praising God. I did not enjoy it. The Sunday School lesson was fine, and I had no quarrel with the worship service that followed; but this corporate praise, led by this woman, consisting largely of mindless ditties with insipid tunes, was intolerable. My brothers, my friends, and I were ruthless and relentless in our cynical and disparaging attitude. But she was equal to our challenge; she made us sing—and being a PK and well aware of the price of public disobedience, I had no option. I sang:

"Allelu, allelu, allelu, alleluia! Praise ye the Lord!"

You know how it went. Standing up. Sitting down. Singing it louder so that the grown-ups gathered in the "overflow room" for Bible class could hear us, we belted out our praises to God. In spite of us, Mrs. G. taught all of us—taught *me*—how to praise God.

She won.

Of course, I did not realize it at the time. Actually, I probably didn't fully realize it until just a few days ago, as the task of working through this study and thinking about the praise of God jogged my memory and took me back to those Sunday mornings so long ago. The discomfort, the embarrassment, and even the less-than-exemplary attitude have all faded into insignificance. Now, the memory makes me smile. And now I recognize that during those agonizingly long Sunday School openings a valuable habit was being imprinted on me and formed into my very being. I learned on those Sunday mornings that a man praises God not because he feels like it, but because he must. Yes, I am quite serious about this: praise has next to nothing to do with feelings and just about everything to do with being a creature, who recognizes a creature's obligation to praise his Creator. This is the lesson I learned on those Sunday mornings because no matter how I felt inside, my mouth would form the words and I would sing God's praise. Mrs. G. made sure of it. Without realizing it, I learned then that you praise God not because you feel like it, but because you're supposed to—and that's a very good lesson to learn.

Feelings are tremendously over-rated, of course. A man's feelings can drive him into shameful, faithless actions. A man's feelings can corrupt his judgment. A man's feelings can endorse the most foolhardy choices. Of course, it's not that feelings are somehow evil or harmful. Feelings can also be beneficial and occasionally may actually lead to right action or help reinforce right thinking . . . "gut feelings" and that sort of thing. It's just that feelings are not particularly reliable. Feelings do not provide a legitimate foundation for thinking or acting . . . or praising God. That's the real point that I learned from Mrs. G. One does not wait for his feelings to be right before he does right. A Christian does not restrict his praise of God only to those times when he feels like praising God. Yes, it's great to have feelings that support your actions, and it is certainly easier to do the right thing when you feel like doing the right thing. But, having those right feelings doesn't necessarily make the right actions any better or even more meaningful. For whatever reason, we associate the praise of God with happy, exuberant feelings, or at the very least with just a little enthusiasm—"Sing it like you mean it!" Praise of God, though, cannot become dependent on feelings, nor is it enhanced by the presence or the absence of one feeling or another. Feelings are feelings and praise of God is praise of God; and the two are quite independent of one another.

Of course, this lesson on what makes praise count as good praise puts those often-maligned liturgical alleluias in quite a different light as well. It may seem a bit incongruous to call it "praise" when a congregation of worshipers reads a scripted litany that concludes with a triple alleluia. Admittedly, the dispassionate and disinterested monotone that typically issues from the congregation with diminishing volume—"Alleluia . . . alleluia . . . alleluia . . . "—may not sound the way we think praise should sound, but perhaps the problem is not with the congregation or the litany, but with our assumptions about what praise is supposed to be.

When it comes to exploring more fully what it means to praise God, it is quite fitting and wise, albeit painfully predictable, that we turn to the Psalms. We expect the Psalms to be filled with insights into how one should praise God. The Psalms even supply concrete, ready-made prayers of praise waiting to be pressed anew into service. And the psalms considered in this volume do not disappoint. Praise is the central theme. These psalms reflect on the practice of praise, they demonstrate praise, and they encourage praise.

In the pages that follow, you will delve into a study that, if successful, will lead you to rethink some of the things you have assumed about what it means to praise God. But it will probably do much more than that. Guided by stories of personal discovery as told by men not unlike yourself, you will discover and reaffirm truths that impact much more than your understanding and practice of praise. In fact, you may be surprised at how much a study on "psalms of praise" is able to teach you about ordinary, regular life—the life you live from Sunday afternoon through Saturday night. The men who penned the devotions that make up this volume have much to teach you about many things. You will learn about the challenge of handling success, the bold face of Christian courage in the corporate boardroom, the danger of pride and self-confidence when God blesses you with success, the responsibility of shaping a meaningful legacy for your heirs, the power of a father to form a son, the reality of living life on the edge of the pit of death and despair, the wonder of yielding to God's work in creating and saving you. This study is about more than learning how to sing a praise chorus. It is about more than getting your feelings right. It is about discovering what it means to be a man of God who lives his life as praise to his Creator.

Certainly, the best studies are those that do more than impart information or generate insights. The best studies change those who are studying so that they become different—and yes, *better*—people. You will read the stories of men who have been changed by what they learned; but until what you learn changes you, this study has fallen short. In other words, the goal is that you do more than merely read. The goal is that you do more than merely read and reflect. The goal is that you do more than merely read, reflect, and discuss. The goal is that you do more than merely read, reflect, discuss, and pray. The goal is that you read, reflect, discuss, pray . . . and *change*. This happens when what you study—God's Word—enters into your thinking and reshapes your entire worldview. This happens when what you study becomes what you are. Such transformation of your thinking and your being may occur in a sudden burst—a piercing conviction, a re-creating confession, a renewed life. Or, as in my case through a childhood of routine Sunday School openings, it may be a deliberate and methodical renewal of the person that, when complete, is no less dramatic for its slower pace. However it happens, it happens: God makes the change.

The first volume of this series began with my exhortation: "Read the Psalms." While that is still good counsel, I've concluded that it is altogether inadequate. One can read without undergoing transformation. One can read without the words entering the thinking and the being of the person. Simply skimming the Psalms will not accomplish the goal of a changed life. What is needed is an appropriation of the truth of the Psalms that happens when the words, the wisdom, the laments, the hope, the prayers, the praise of the Psalms become those of the present reader. What is needed is that the words enter into and become part of *you*. Do more than read, reflect, discuss, and pray. Alone, and with a group of friends, encounter the Psalms, enter the Psalms, and engage the Psalms, because in them, God is encountering, entering, and engaging you.

Week One

Psalm 40

[1] I waited patiently for the LORD;
He inclined to me and heard my cry.

[2] He drew me up from the pit of destruction,
out of the miry bog,
and set my feet upon a rock,
making my steps secure.

[3] He put a new song in my mouth,
a song of praise to our God.
Many will see and fear,
and put their trust in the LORD.

[4] Blessed is the man who makes
the LORD his trust,
who does not turn to the proud,
to those who go astray after a lie!

[5] You have multiplied, O LORD my God,
Your wondrous deeds and Your thoughts toward us;
none can compare with You!
I will proclaim and tell of them,
yet they are more than can be told.

[6] In sacrifice and offering You have not delighted,
but You have given me an open ear.
Burnt offering and sin offering
You have not required.

[7] Then I said, "Behold, I have come;
in the scroll of the book it is written of me:

[8] I delight to do Your will, O my God;
Your law is within my heart."

[9] I have told the glad news of deliverance
in the great congregation;

behold, I have not restrained my lips,
as You know, O Lord.

10 I have not hidden Your deliverance within my heart;
I have spoken of Your faithfulness and Your salvation;
I have not concealed Your steadfast love and Your faithfulness
from the great congregation.

11 As for You, O Lord, You will not restrain
Your mercy from me;
Your steadfast love and Your faithfulness will
ever preserve me!

12 For evils have encompassed me
beyond number;
my iniquities have overtaken me,
and I cannot see;
they are more than the hairs of my head;
my heart fails me.

13 Be pleased, O Lord, to deliver me!
O Lord, make haste to help me!

14 Let those be put to shame and disappointed altogether
who seek to snatch away my life;
let those be turned back and brought to dishonor
who delight in my hurt!

15 Let those be appalled because of their shame
who say to me, "Aha, Aha!"

16 But may all who seek You
rejoice and be glad in You;
may those who love Your salvation
say continually, "Great is the Lord!"

17 As for me, I am poor and needy,
but the Lord takes thought for me.
You are my help and my deliverer;
do not delay, O my God!

Joe Hanson

Psalm 40:1-3

> I waited patiently for the LORD; He inclined to me and heard
> my cry. He drew me up from the pit of destruction, out of the
> miry bog, and set my feet upon a rock, making my steps secure.
> He put a new song in my mouth, a song of praise to our God.
> Many will see and fear, and put their trust in the LORD.

Out of the Pit

I've put a guy or two into a slimy pit. One of them was even a four-star admiral wearing his dress blue uniform, medals and all. You'd think they would have resisted, or at least voiced an objection, but nobody made a peep. They were dead as doornails. Being dead is the primary qualification for being the guest of honor at a Navy funeral. Every time I ever served on a funeral detail or honor guard, whether there was a big brass band or just a sobbing young widow with a crying baby, the program always ended by putting someone into the slimy pit. As far as I know, they're all still in there, waiting patiently.

Psalm 40 talks about getting out of the pit. If I were in a slimy pit, you can be sure I'd have dirt under my fingernails before I gave up trying. I'd figure out something. I'd be resourceful. I'd check my pockets for makeshift escape tools. I'd make a plan. And I'd holler my head off. Unless, of course, I were dead, because I'm nothing if not resourceful.

So what does this have to do with the "I waited patiently" guy in the psalm? It means he was a goner and he knew it. It means that waiting was the only thing he was capable of doing. His patience is not remarkable, it's inevitable. There's no way he can get out of the pit on his own. He can't even assist with a rescue. God does it all. The guy in the pit isn't thrown a rope or given a hand. No one pokes a branch at him to grab or offers a piece of encouraging advice. He is simply lifted out.

It reminds me of watching a friend who was working down in a slimy pit one day, laying sewer pipe in the rain. Without warning, in an instant, the muddy walls of the trench sagged and then collapsed around him. Wet clay packed him in up to his chin. He was as good as dead if left to his own devices. He didn't scream or yell. He turned his head and simply looked up at his partner who leaped off his backhoe, right into the pit. Digging furiously and carefully with bare hands, he uncovered my friend, dragged him free, and got him back up on solid ground again.

That's God's specialty—getting right down into the pit. Although my first inclination is to think that Psalm 40 is about me, I haven't gone to Bible study all these years just for the weak decaf and doughnuts. So I know that, as usual, the psalm is pointing toward Jesus. He takes my pit and gives me His rock to stand on. The slimy pit is more than just a bad day at the office. It's hell down there. But that's God for you. He lifts me out, sets me straight, and takes my place. My contribution is nothing, zip.

I remember when my kids were very young, they'd sometimes make a big mess—break something, spill something, get something all mixed up. And then, half out of guilt, hoping to escape punishment—or maybe from naive self-confidence—they'd try to help with the cleanup. Often their efforts were useless, in the way, and sometimes they made things worse.

Feeling useless, being helpless, doesn't come easily to me or most guys I know. In fact, it's un-American. We prefer Yankee ingenuity and self-starters who get ahead on their own. Often I work with managers and executives who come from various countries in Asia to work in the U.S. office of their American employers. A tough part of their transition is adjusting to our do-it-yourself culture. It's difficult for them to accept our self-service attitude or understand why do-it-yourselfers are admired. But that same attitude makes it easy for me to forget that I haven't contributed anything to my own rescue or to talk about it objectively, after the fact.

Even my own prayers and songs are pretty self-centered, and the harder I try to improve them, the worse they get. But this psalm reminds me not to worry about it. God takes them all and gives me a "new song" and a "song of praise." Remember Jonah? He's a favorite of mine. Talk about being in a slimy pit! Dead as a mackerel, Jonah wastes no energy working on his escape. He spends his whale time singing a song that he only could have gotten from God. "You brought up my life from the pit," he says (Jonah 2:6). "Salvation belongs to the LORD!" (v. 9). As I've grown older, I've learned to love the liturgy more and more because I realize it relieves me of finding the right things to say and sing. Instead, we give up our ideas and use the words God has given us for worship. Sitting in church, I might as well be inside a whale or on the edge of the pit, singing my head off.

Even back on terra firma, however, everybody has a bad day at the office—and much worse. These days, when someone says "I'm in the hole," we know they're talking about pay dirt, finances, being underground financially. "I'm in over my head" means "I feel overwhelmed." Some folks say "I'm down in the dumps." Maybe that's not a slimy pit, but a situation that challenges or threatens or wears us down. Each Sunday our Prayer of the Church names members who need help—Wayne, Larry, Janet, Thomas, Lorraine, and more. Psalm 40 is for these pits as well as the big one. It doesn't promise to fill up my bank account or cure Ted's illness or make Ed's job less stressful. But it assures me that I don't need to go through any of those things alone. If Jesus is willing to take our spot in the pit—if God "did not spare His own Son . . . will He not also with Him graciously give us all things?" (Romans 8:32).

Advent had just begun when I started thinking about Psalm 40. The "waiting patiently" part seemed poignant and seasonal. I thought about hope and faith and how important they are when someone goes through a period of trouble or hardship. Then Baby Jesus came and went, and soon it was Lent. I realized how much further the psalm had to take me and that Someone suffered hell on the cross in my place. But Jesus wasn't left in His pit, the cold and darkened tomb. "God raised Him up, loosing the pangs of death" (Acts 2:24), and the stone was rolled away from the pit on Easter. That's the rock He sets our feet on, and it's the Easter rock that makes the new song worth singing. It's the reason to "see and fear and put their trust in the LORD" (Psalm 40:3).

I realized how much further the psalm had to take me and that Someone suffered hell on the cross in my place. But Jesus wasn't left in His pit, the cold and darkened tomb. "God raised Him up, loosing the pangs of death" (Acts 2:24).

Prayer: Heavenly Father, sometimes I find myself stuck in a slimy pit, a pit of my own choosing. Thank You for sending Jesus, who rescued me from the ultimate pit of sin, Satan, and death. Grant that through my humble praise, others might put their trust in You. I ask this through Christ, my Lord. Amen.

Monday

DAILY STUDY QUESTIONS
Psalm 40:1-3

1. What sort of slimy pits have been causing you trouble recently?

2. Why is it good to remember that the *definitive* slimy pit that traps us is the grave?

3. Why is patient waiting the one absolute prerequisite for Christian discipleship?

4. What excuses might a person offer to shield himself from having to learn the humble art of patient waiting?

5. What tangible difference will God's promised work of rescuing make in your life today?

Psalm 40:4–5

> Blessed is the man who makes the LORD his trust, who does not turn to the proud, to those who go astray after a lie! You have multiplied, O LORD my God, Your wondrous deeds and Your thoughts toward us; none can compare with You! I will proclaim and tell of them, yet they are more than can be told.

Trust in the Lord

Blessed is the wide receiver with six catches and two touchdowns. Blessed is the power forward with the triple double in game 7 of the playoffs. Blessed is the MVP. Blessed is the southpaw with the complete-game shutout.

Everybody feels blessed these days. It makes me cringe. The game is over and the sideline reporter, Sally Jean, nabs the hero of the winning team for a quick interview. "Well, Darren, they couldn't find a way to stop you in the final period today." "I feel blessed," says Darren.

"Blessed" sounds out of place when I hear it from a guy with a number on his shirt and a towel around his neck. I squirm a little when the interview begins that way. I can't tell if Darren is saying that he's grateful for God's gift of speed, or if he is trying to sound modest about his accomplishments, or if he's happy to be a winner. Maybe it's just a sophisticated way to say, "I'm lucky."

Sally Jean never follows up. Maybe she's uncomfortable too. The exchange shifts to what his coach said to him or what his strategy was or the statistics themselves. Blessed are the winners. Losers never feel blessed. Does that sound right? I realize I have a lot more to learn and understand about being blessed. Or is it "blest"? Usually by this time, I hit the mute button or surf to a game on another channel.

Here in Psalm 40, the guy from the pit tells us who is blessed. It's the "man who makes the LORD his trust" (v. 4). He's talking about himself, of course. When he was in the pit, he did nothing—nothing but wait patiently for the One he trusted. He trusted Someone on whom he could rely. He trusted Someone who could save him. His blessing was God's act of salvation. God raised Jesus from the dead. And because

He takes my place in the pit, I can trust Him to raise me too.

Blessing often gets mixed up with good luck. But like trust, it's a gift.

Apparently, then, being blessed is not about winning or losing—it's about trusting. In fact, the psalm doesn't say that blessing is a feeling, but rather something that we become. That's a relief. If being blessed depended on how I felt, I'd miss out pretty frequently. God's blessing depends on Him, not me.

Trust is rare these days, and loss of trust is more of a daily occurrence than encountering a blessed athlete. Trust, which I formerly took for granted, is fading away. My friends feel the same way I do about elected politicians who turn out to be corrupt and completely self-serving; leaders of blue-chip companies who fleece their investors and abuse the people who work for them; pastors and priests who take advantage of the office to hurt the very people who need their help; investment advisers who don't tell the truth—at least, not the *whole* truth; and athletes and celebrities who get their "blessings" from a needle. It's hard to trust anyone anymore.

The psalmist teaches me that I have a choice about whom I trust: "the Lord," or egotists and liars. When a choice is either God first or someone else, things boil down to First Commandment stuff. It's about idolatry. The word *idolatry* hasn't crept out of its old-fashioned church context into popular vocabulary the way *blessing* has.

Too bad. I could frequently use a reminder about the biggest idol of them all. When I'm in a jam, the Little Red Hen in me often looks to myself first for help. My natural tendency when I'm in deep trouble is to trust myself. The psalmist sets things up simply for me. It's an either/or choice—the Lord or "other." He says it's either faith or idolatry. Making the wrong choice is its own reward—no blessing.

After being rescued from the pit, a new man emerges, so he changes his tune and sings a new song. Jesus, who teaches us this new song, first teaches us how to trust God. Especially in His prayer in the Garden of Gethsemane (Matthew 26, John 17), the evening before He entered the pit, He laid out His choices: trust His human feelings (specifically His fear of what His Passion would entail) or trust His Father. Then He chose to trust God's plan, not only for Himself, but also for me. In that same prayer, He also entrusts His disciples and all believers to God and asks that God not only raise them up to where He is going, but that His Father will give them the joy He knows.

Verses 4 and 5 of Psalm 40 are the prelude of the new song. They make two comparisons. First, we hear that God can be trusted and that the blessings follow from Him. This choice is compared with the consequence of trusting anyone else and therefore going astray. When we go astray instead of being blessed, we are likely to wind up back in the pit or at least get our feet muddy. The lyrics also compare God's deeds and thoughts to my capacity to fathom them all. In both comparisons, I come up short on my own.

Verse 5 of the psalm makes me think it was written especially for Americans—especially sports fans like me. Is there a country in the world that likes making lists more than we do? We always want to count things, rank things, and add them up. A "top ten" list is irresistible, and a "top hundred" is even better. Even the best sports-trivia nuts I know don't know it all, but that doesn't keep them from going on and on. The guy in the psalm can't resist making a list either, even though he admits it will be inadequate. That's the magnitude of God's blessing, and that's the magnitude of its effect on him.

Proud people trust themselves, sing the same old song about themselves, and discover sooner or later that do-it-yourself blessings are illusions that lead them astray. The man who is otherwise hopeless but trusts God discovers that God does it all, including giving him something new and limitless to sing about. To top it all off, He gives us Jesus, who shows us the perfect example of trust that He likewise gives us by His grace.

After being rescued from the pit, a new man emerges, so he changes his tune and sings a new song. Jesus, who teaches us this new song, first teaches us how to trust God.

Prayer: Lord God, I confess my own pride in my accomplishments. For the sake of Jesus, please forgive me, strengthen my trust in You, and help me to focus on Your wondrous deeds that You accomplish through me and through others by Your grace. In Jesus' name. Amen.

Tuesday

DAILY STUDY QUESTIONS
Psalm 40:4–5

1. What's a favorite "Top Ten" or "Top Hundred" that you like to monitor from time to time?

2. Suppose you started to follow through on David's plan and began to list the wonders that God has done specifically on your own behalf. What would you include in your Top Ten?

3. Why is it a good idea actually to sit down and recount the wonders God has done for you?

4. In what situations do you find it most difficult to put your trust in the Lord?

5. In what sense is it right that one has only two choices: either trust in God, or trust in proud liars?

Psalm 40:6–11

> In sacrifice and offering You have not delighted, but You have given me an open ear. Burnt offering and sin offering You have not required. Then I said, "Behold, I have come; in the scroll of the book it is written of me: I delight to do Your will, O my God; Your law is within my heart." I have told the glad news of deliverance in the great congregation; behold, I have not restrained my lips, as You know, O Lord. I have not hidden Your deliverance within my heart; I have spoken of Your faithfulness and Your salvation; I have not concealed Your steadfast love and Your faithfulness from the great congregation. As for You, O Lord, You will not restrain Your mercy from me; Your steadfast love and Your faithfulness will ever preserve me!

Listen to Him

Imagine a pig all laid out on a stretcher with a handle at each corner so it can be carried easily. There's a piece of fruit in the pig's mouth, and pineapples, oranges, and an apple or two around the carcass. Bowls of rice, cups of rice wine, and sticks of burning incense are arranged on the little platform as well. After a parade through the streets with horns and gongs attracting spectators, the magnificent sacrifice winds up at the temple at the idol's feet. I've seen it many times in my travels in Asia, especially in smaller towns and communities. I can assure you that the idols never smile, say thanks, or show any appreciation for all the fuss. That's divine gratitude for you.

Trying to make God happy can be a full-time job. People have spent a lot of time at it, whether they live in an Asian village or in a high-rise Western condo. Sometimes they do it to get on God's good side in order to get blessings. Or they do it to make up and compensate for doing things they know have displeased Him. It's the ultimate application of the do-it-yourself mentality, and it's the ultimate waste of time. But the man who took my place in the pit in Psalm 40 is up to something different. He's singing about all that God has done to make *him* happy.

He understands that empty rituals don't impress God. He knows "it is impossible for the blood of bulls and goats to take away sins" (Hebrews 10:4). Being in the pit is an impossible situation because anything I might do, and any sacrifice I might come up with, would be futile. On the other hand, God's Law required sacrifices—in fact, lots of them. Old Testament priests made sacrifices over and over again, every day through the centuries. The Law also said that sacrifices must be perfect or they were not acceptable. "You shall not offer anything that has a blemish, for it will not be acceptable for you. And when anyone offers a sacrifice of peace offerings to the Lord to fulfill a vow or as a freewill offering from the herd or from the flock, to be accepted it must be perfect; there shall be no blemish in it" (Leviticus 22:20–21).

The contradiction is a tough one for me to crack. The new song celebrates the good news that my sacrifices are not good enough; in fact, they're not any good at all! God resolves the dilemma, and this is the key to the rest of the song. God accepted imperfect sacrifices if they were made trusting His mercy, not trying to impress Him. Sacrifices were made looking forward in faith to the perfect sacrifice that God, who does it all, would provide on the cross. Jesus Himself is the only perfect sacrifice.

Remember verse 4 of the psalm: "Blessed is the man who makes the Lord his trust." Blessing follows from trust in God's sacrifice, not our own efforts.

Trust is not only rare; God knows we can't come up with it on our own. So besides giving us Jesus' perfect example, He goes further and gives us the gift of faith. The blessed man says that God has thought of everything and has "given [him] an open ear" (Psalm 40:6). My open ears please God rather than my sacrifices because through them I learn to trust Him. God speaks His Word through my open ears, and the Holy Spirit uses that Word to create faith. Now, instead of trying to satisfy God with my sacrifices and offerings apart from faith, I can please Him by trusting His Son who lived a perfect life for me and suffered for me on the cross until God raised Him from the pit of death. There is absolutely nothing left for me to do to receive His blessing. Now, through faith, my sacrifices and offerings please Him, not in order to receive, but as an expression of gratefulness.

The new song is about Jesus. The new song tells us that He is the one who fulfills God's promise. "Behold, I have come; in the scroll of the book it is written of me: I delight to do Your will, O my God" (Psalm 40:7–8). The new song is sung about Him "in the great congregation." Everyone everywhere will know that God is the only Savior. The ones with mere rituals and good works and sacrifices are the ones whom verse 4 called the "proud" who go astray.

When "the great congregation" hears the new song, something else happens. Back in verse 3 it says that "many will see and fear, and put their trust in the Lord."

Even though the new song can't completely recount everything that God has done for me, it's important for others in a pit to hear it so they will trust God too. John's Gospel says that Jesus did much more than is recorded, but those things that were recorded were "written so that you may believe that Jesus is the Christ, the Son of God, and that by believing you may have life in His name" (John 20:31).

Ears are not just for hearing, but for learning. Isaiah says, "Morning by morning He awakens; He awakens my ear to hear as those who are taught" (Isaiah 50:4). Even though there is nothing left that I must do, there is plenty for me to learn. Jesus made this point to the Pharisees when He recited this psalm to them in Matthew 9. He said, "Go and learn what this means, 'I desire mercy, and not sacrifice.' For I came not to call the righteous, but sinners" (v. 13). My trust is renewed and becomes stronger as I hear His Word.

My trust becomes stronger as I hear the new song over again because I have more to learn, not only about what He has done for me, but about the mercy that He shows to those who "are sick." Verse 11 of the Psalm says that God does "not restrain [His] mercy" from me, nor from anyone who trusts Him. I confess that I often judge other people by the quality of their sacrifices and rituals rather than by the wonderful things that God has done for them.

God says He loves mercy more than sacrifice. He sent Jesus to show us His mercy and give us His eternal blessing. What pleases Him? Not mere sacrifices, rituals, or even good works. He says plainly in Matthew 17:5, "This is My beloved Son, with whom I am well pleased; listen to Him." God is pleased with His Son, and He is pleased with us when we listen to His Son with God-given faith. That faith infuses the sacrifice of our lives, our worship, and our good works so that they are truly pleasing to God. The blessed man trusts Jesus and listens to Him.

My open ears please God rather than my sacrifices because through them I learn to trust Him. God speaks His Word through my open ears, and the Holy Spirit uses that Word to create faith.

Prayer: Blessed Holy Spirit, forgive me for blocking my ears to Your Word about Christ through poor church attendance and infrequent Bible study and devotion. By Your grace, open my ears once more so that I might serve God by faith and my neighbor by love. In Jesus' name. Amen.

Wednesday

DAILY STUDY QUESTIONS
Psalm 40:6–11

1. What's the biggest sacrifice you can recall making for another person?

2. What kind of sacrifices or offerings does God expect you to make?

3. Who is the "I" that is the subject of these verses?

4. What responsibility to his fellow creatures does the psalmist acknowledge?

5. It is fairly obvious how God's loving kindness preserves you, but how does God's truth also preserve you?

Psalm 40:12-16

For evils have encompassed me beyond number; my iniquities have overtaken me, and I cannot see; they are more than
the hairs of my head; my heart fails me. Be pleased, O Lord, to
deliver me! O Lord, make haste to help me! Let those be put to
shame and disappointed altogether who seek to snatch away
my life; let those be turned back and brought to dishonor who
delight in my hurt! Let those be appalled because of their
shame who say to me, "Aha, Aha!" But may all who seek You
rejoice and be glad in You; may those who love Your salvation
say continually, "Great is the Lord!"

One All-time Hit Song

Tunes can take over. Especially tunes without words. A bit of music will start running through my head and I lose control of it. I can't get the tune out of my head once it starts. It's as if it's programmed in my brain on a continuous loop. Sometimes it's a melody I enjoy. Sometimes it's only a jingle from a TV commercial. If I can recall the words that go with the notes, that usually stops the distraction. When I can't come up with the lyrics, the music gets old very quickly, and my efforts to find the words are frustrating.

It seems as if verses 12–16 of Psalm 40 are the lyrics to the "new song" that the man from the pit is singing. This is the guy who "waited patiently" in verse 1. He couldn't have come up with these words on his own. The song not only tells us that he's in deep trouble, but that he can't even fathom how bad his situation is— surrounded and outpaced, according to verse 12: "For evils have encompassed me beyond number; my iniquities have overtaken me." The words also suggest that he is already singing this anthem while he is still in the pit, waiting for God to rescue him.

During the Vietnam War, I remember hearing about prisoners who spent time in their cells singing. I don't recall that they composed any songs of their own, however. They sang the songs they were given—songs they learned in Sunday School and church, maybe songs their moms had taught them. Singing can make time pass more easily. Like the man in the pit, all they could do was wait patiently.

No atheists in foxholes, they say. Apparently what takes place in the pits, however, is battlefield negotiations with God: "If You get me out of this, God, I'm gonna clean up my act. You can count on it." Or "I hope You remember that I've been pretty good, Lord, and that You'll help me to survive this." Maybe best of all are the stories about hopeless cases that vow to go to seminary (or at least attend church every Sunday) in exchange for God's rescue.

You don't have to be in a foxhole—or in a pit of destruction—to behave this way. Lesser dilemmas sometimes make me engage in the same type of bargaining. Lost car keys? "God, if You do this, I'll do that." Somebody sick? In an airplane in a thunderstorm? You know how it goes. In America, we are leashed to "cause and effect" reasoning. I like to believe that I can affect my destiny by what I do. It's almost scientific! Even when I can't control a situation, sometimes I try to control God. The psalmist has no such illusions. He waits patiently. He's singing while he waits, but not his own song. He brings nothing to the situation. On his own, he knows he's a goner. "My heart fails me," he says. I think I already mentioned that he is dead.

What's he singing about? What's the song he was given? First of all, he has a math problem. He has so many sins that he can't count them all. "Evils have encompassed me beyond number," he sings in verse 12. The song leaves no doubt that the singer has no way out. Surrounded and overtaken, he says. No loopholes. He can sing about it because he knows that when it comes to sins, God doesn't count, either. The singer is blessed because he is forgiven. It reminds me of God's promise in this regard: "If You, O Lord, should mark iniquities, O Lord, who could stand?" (Psalm 130:3). The worse things are for him, the greater the blessing he has received.

The song goes on. "I can't see a thing," he sings. "I'm blinded by my sins. It's like having my hair in my eyes." It's an interesting way of thinking of things. Sin blinds us. What is it that he can't see? His own predicament? A way to escape? At this point, he can't see his God, his Savior. After Adam and Eve's sin had overtaken them in the garden, they hid themselves from God. How can anyone come to God on his own if he can't see Him? God always comes to sinners, not the other way around. This passage also makes me think of Jesus, who took my place on the cross. When He was covered with my sins, He also could not see His Father. He could only ask, "My God, why have You forsaken Me?"

Having recited the man's hopeless sinful condition, the lyrics of the new song proclaim the refrain in verse 13. "Be pleased, O Lord, to deliver me! O Lord, make haste to help me!" The blessing is in the promise. The promise does not depend on me—and that's why it's dependable. The song goes, "Be pleased, O Lord, to deliver me!" God doesn't save me reluctantly. He hasn't been talked into it. He doesn't owe it to me because of anything I've done. He isn't giving to me as advance compensation for something I've promised to do.

God always does what pleases Him. God Himself is happy to save me. That explains why He always makes the first move. When I feel blessed, I'm really sharing in the happiness that He feels by keeping His promise and restoring me to life again.

The lyrics continue and point at those who persecute the singer. They mock him because of his plight, and perhaps even more because of his faith. He's in the hole, singing his lungs out, and they don't get it, so they laugh. They're Noah's neighbors hooting at him for climbing into his dark boat. They're the folks who look at me and wonder how someone as imperfect as I am can expect anything at all from God. The singer and I have the last "Aha!" because we can always expect God to do what He pleases. What kind of blessing would it be and what kind of song would it be if they came without some laughter?

This is what the second refrain in verse 16 is all about. It says that blessing and happiness are sharing God's happiness. God takes my pit and gives me His rock to stand on. He takes my situation without a future and gives me a promise that when people see what He is planning for me, they will know how great He is. And He takes my wordless jingles and gives me words and music to the number one all-time hit song that goes on and on and on.

....

God doesn't save me reluctantly. He hasn't been talked into it. He doesn't owe it to me because of anything I've done. He isn't giving to me as advance compensation for something I've promised to do. God always does what pleases Him.

Prayer: Lord Jesus Christ, sometimes it seems my sins surround me and won't let me out of the pit of guilt and despair. During those times, rescue me, cleanse me of unrighteousness, and lift me up with Your strong hands that still bear the marks of Calvary. I ask this in Your name. Amen.

....

Thursday

DAILY STUDY QUESTIONS
Psalm 40:12-16

1. Recall a time when your sins caught up with you.

2. How does Satan use the size and number of your sins to keep you from seeing clearly?

3. What is the relationship between verses 12 and 13?

4. Is God ever *not* pleased to rescue His desperate servant? Does He ever tire of the task? How does God's disposition of mercy and grace affect your living today?

5. Throughout this section, David is explicit in his desire for God to act speedily. Why might God make you wait for Him to step in with His work of deliverance?

Psalm 40:17

As for me, I am poor and needy, but the Lord takes thought for me. You are my help and my deliverer; do not delay, O my God!

Come, Lord Jesus

Did you ever hear of the "Olympic Beatitudes"? What about Beijing 2008? I didn't go to the games, but shortly before they began, I saw the beatitudes plastered around the stadiums and arenas in the northern district of the city. It wasn't necessary to visit the structures in Beijing, however, to see Beibei, Jingjing, Huanhuan, Yingying, and Nini. Wherever I traveled in China, I saw images of these official mascots of the Olympic Games on billboards, TV ads, key rings, chopsticks, and stuffed toys. They were much more than promotions for the 2008 Olympics, however. They were symbols of the "Five Blessings" in traditional Chinese culture. These blessings are received by practicing the same virtues that lead to gold medals—hard work, fair and goodwill. Oh, and lots of luck.

As I read the last verse of Psalm 40—"I am poor and needy"—the blessings of Jesus, the Beatitudes in Matthew 5, come to my mind. "Blessed are the poor in spirit," Jesus says (v. 3). Blessings are for losers. Jesus explains what the singer in Psalm 40 is talking about. He does not mention possessions. He is not out to condemn large bank accounts, season tickets to the White Sox, or riding lawn mowers. He doesn't suggest that there is virtue in being down and out. It's not what we have but who we are that matters. The "poor and needy" guy is a loser.

Jesus hangs out with losers. This includes folks with money. He was criticized because "many tax collectors and sinners came and were reclining with Jesus and His disciples" (Matthew 9:10). They had money, but they were still poor and needy.

They had broken all the rules. They had made enemies of everyone. Some of them were regarded as traitors. Their blessing is in His promise. It has nothing to do with prosperity, happiness, passion, health, and good luck, the traditional Chinese "beatitudes." He says, "I came not to call the righteous, but sinners" (Matthew 9:13).

Some of my non-Christian friends criticize Jesus for hanging out with the wrong sort of people. He doesn't live up to their expectations when it comes to whom He lets into the Church and, down the road, into heaven. It's as if He doesn't have any standards. These friends like to point out all the hypocrites that belong to the Church. They're quick to point out people who don't follow the rules God has laid out. Losers don't deserve blessings. It's not fair. What use is it to be a good Christian if some church members are losers? But that's God for you. Jesus says, "I desire mercy, and not sacrifice" (Matthew 9:13).

Jesus spends His time showing mercy. The singer in Psalm 40 qualifies for God's mercy because he's poor and needy. He has absolutely no redeeming qualities of his own. We already know he's rotten to the core and surrounded and overtaken by evil (Psalm 40:12). God lifts him out of the pit and Jesus takes his place in the hole. The losers in the pews at my church and I receive the same blessing because we know we are poor and needy and all we can do is depend on God to show us His mercy.

Being poor and needy qualifies me for mercy, but how do I know that's the condition I'm in? Like the psalmist, I can't see or measure how bad things are. We're both blind as bats. No one wants to be blind, especially about himself. However, what people usually talk about is not their blindness but their blind spots—obstructions to their vision here and there. No one is ready to say they are completely in the dark. They believe all they need is a little help—not a rescue. Folks feel that if they have a good self-analysis, then they will know what to do and how to adapt in order to get ahead, compete effectively, and solve their problems. They spend a lot of time taking personal inventories or paying someone to do it for them. The results never say "bankrupt," however, much less "dead as a doornail." I enjoy looking at all the self-help books on the shelves at my favorite bookstores and wondering why so many are needed. If they're not enough, apparently there's free advice to be had as well, from experts such as Oprah and Dr. Phil, although I haven't watched them on TV myself (really!). Even if they would tell me I have nothing at all worth saving, their remedies would never be enough.

The psalmist shows me the way to the sight and insight I need. It's a gift. The psalmist is given a "new song," and the lyrics describe his plight. He understands that his only hope is to wait patiently for God to save him. Similarly, the psalm points us toward Jesus, who goes around giving sight to the blind so that we can see how much we need Him.

God gives me His Word. Like the new song, it points me to Jesus who shows me what God is like, and who promises to make a trade with me—my poorness and shortcomings in exchange for His rich blessing and mercy. The only yardstick for how poor I am is by comparison with God Himself and how rich He is. The blessing is that He's willing to give it all away to those who trust Him. Jesus says, "All that the Father has is Mine; therefore I said that He will take what is Mine and declare it to you" (John 16:15). Why should He do this? Back in verse 13, the song says it is because it pleases Him. We know that "without faith it is impossible to please Him, for whoever would draw near to God must believe that He exists and that He rewards those who seek Him" (Hebrews 11:6). Trusting God is linked to being poor and needy, and it is the reason He blesses us.

The song promises that in spite of my own lack of awareness of myself and of God, He is aware of me. The "Lord takes thought of me," it promises (v. 17). God not only does everything; He thinks of everything. And He always acts first. I'm reminded of this during the Lord's Supper at church. Members who are blind or otherwise unable to come to the altar wait patiently in their pews. The pastors bring the Sacrament to those members where they sit. What a picture of the ultimate blessing—not good luck, not good health or any of the other Olympic Beatitudes. God takes our cheap blessings that we try to achieve by hard work and behaving ourselves, and especially by winning, and He gives us a blessing we can really sing about. The blessing is Jesus Himself who comes to me when I cannot come to Him. Come, Lord Jesus!

....

God takes our cheap blessings that we try to achieve by hard work and behaving ourselves, and especially by winning, and He gives us a blessing we can really sing about.

Prayer: Lord Jesus Christ, You call the poor in spirit "blessed." Take the poverty of my sins and restore me to the full status of being Your brother, a son of Your heavenly Father, and the riches of His mercy and grace. I ask this in Your name. Amen.

....

Friday

DAILY STUDY QUESTIONS
Psalm 40:17

1. What are some virtues or blessings that you have been trying to add to your life lately?

2. According to the psalm's final verse, what is the one essential criterion for God to give His blessing?

3. How does a person go about becoming afflicted and needy (a loser!) so that he will be in the right place to receive God's gift?

4. David calls God his "deliverer." From what does God deliver David? From what does He deliver you?

5. How does this final verse provide a shining example of a faith that does not waver or doubt?

Week One

The 40th psalm is a beautiful psalm of prayer in which Christ Himself laments His sufferings and calls for rescue from death. It clearly prophesies that He alone does God's will and fulfills the Law, and that this is written about Him in the book of Moses. Christ dissolves and abolishes the old Law of sacrifices and its holiness by which God's will was not fulfilled. God alone does everything for us; nothing is done by our work or sacrifices. He therefore promises and establishes the New Testament in which the justification of the believers will be preached in the great congregation, that is, in the entire world, and not the justification by sacrifices or our works. For works and sacrifices make only arrogant and false saints whose hope is not in God or in His grace, but in their lies and false holiness.

—Martin Luther

GROUP BIBLE STUDY
(Questions and answers on pp. 181–184.)

1. Think of a time when you had no choice but to wait patiently. What were the circumstances, and how did you handle the situation?

2. "Patient waiting" seems to be the definition of *good disciple*. Why might Christians have a hard time coming to terms with the requirement that they learn and even embrace such patient waiting?

3. In Monday's devotion, the author confessed an increasing appreciation for the liturgy: "I realize it relieves me of finding the right things to say and sing. Instead, we give up our ideas and use the words God has given us for worship." What do you think about this idea? How can it be possible that the liturgy is a "new song"?

4. In verse 4, David asserts God's blessing for the man who "makes the LORD his trust." If faith is something the Holy Spirit must create in each of us (Ephesians 2:8–9), what does David mean by making man the one who does the choosing?

5. What does David mean in verse 6 when he asserts, "In sacrifice and offering You have not delighted. . . . Burnt offering and sin offering You have not required," when, in fact, God had specifically required such sacrifices from His people? Is there a proper place for ritual or sacrifices in the lives of Christians?

6. How does this psalm undergo a sort of metamorphosis from being simply praise to being stunningly messianic? Point out all the parts of the psalm that receive new meaning or significance when read in the context of Christ's life and mission.

7. What is the relationship between sin and seeing (v. 12)? What implications might this truth have for society as well as for families and individuals?

8. What's the difference between seeking God and loving His salvation (v. 16)?

9. How are we able to read (much less pray!) verses 14 and 15 without cringing at words that sound embarrassingly self-serving and, well, . . . vengeful?

10. The last verse of the psalm captures the central theme of the entire psalm. What is the cause-and-effect relationship that seems to be at work in this verse? Why is the first part of this relationship so rarely heard or accepted?

Week Two

Psalm 66

1 Shout for joy to God, all the earth;

2 sing the glory of His name;
give to Him glorious praise!

3 Say to God, "How awesome are Your deeds!
So great is Your power that Your enemies come cringing
to You.

4 All the earth worships You
and sings praises to You;
they sing praises to Your name."
Selah

5 Come and see what God has done:
He is awesome in His deeds toward the children of man.

6 He turned the sea into dry land;
they passed through the river on foot.
There did we rejoice in Him,

7 who rules by His might forever,
whose eyes keep watch on the nations—
let not the rebellious exalt themselves.
Selah

8 Bless our God, O peoples;
let the sound of His praise be heard,

9 who has kept our soul among the living
and has not let our feet slip.

10 For You, O God, have tested us;
You have tried us as silver is tried.

¹¹ You brought us into the net;
You laid a crushing burden on our backs;

¹² You let men ride over our heads;
we went through fire and through water;
yet You have brought us out to a place of abundance.

¹³ I will come into Your house with burnt offerings;
I will perform my vows to You,

¹⁴ that which my lips uttered
and my mouth promised when I was in trouble.

¹⁵ I will offer to You burnt offerings of fattened animals,
with the smoke of the sacrifice of rams;
I will make an offering of bulls and goats.
Selah

¹⁶ Come and hear, all you who fear God,
and I will tell what He has done for my soul.

¹⁷ I cried to Him with my mouth,
and high praise was on my tongue.

¹⁸ If I had cherished iniquity in my heart,
the Lord would not have listened.

¹⁹ But truly God has listened;
He has attended to the voice of my prayer.

²⁰ Blessed be God,
because He has not rejected my prayer
or removed His steadfast love from me!

Michael Zpevak

Psalm 66:1–4

Shout for joy to God, all the earth; sing the glory of His name; give to Him glorious praise! Say to God, "How awesome are Your deeds! So great is Your power that Your enemies come cringing to You. All the earth worships You and sings praises to You; they sing praises to Your name." *Selah*

Shout for Joy

Have you ever praised a work colleague—it doesn't matter if it was a boss or a subordinate—for a job extremely well done? How did you feel? Elated? Happy to be part of his or her team? Looking forward to the next opportunity for him or her to shine? Verses 1–4 of Psalm 66 reflect how we feel about our Lord because of what He has done for us. Remember, God is with us in His name. Because of His deeds of salvation, it is simply impossible for us not to sing the Lord's praises. How blessed we all are, men, to live daily the jubilant, Psalm 66 type of praise to God, who has given us everything. But how can we follow the psalmist's specific examples of praise in the modern-day world?

Psalm 66 wastes no time in explaining to us in detail how we redeemed creatures praise our Lord, beginning with the very first word: "Shout." It doesn't say "Speak" or "Think silently" or "Write in a note." No, the psalmist emphasizes the intensity of our praise. Immediately thereafter, Psalm 66 also provides specifics on how we praise God: "for joy." Finally, still within the first two verses, the psalm also explains unmistakably how we communicate our praise: "sing the glory of His name," making certain that His praise is "glorious." Now, this does not mean that when something good happens in our lives—say, a promotion at work—we have to sing the news as a melody line in front of our colleagues, do a happy dance, or orchestrate a 200-person NCAA Division 1 marching band to play outside our office! Yet, we certainly can joyfully sing and glorify our Lord's saving name and praise Him for His blessings upon us, blessings of every kind.

Whenever we credit God for enabling us to enjoy a business achievement or any other type of accomplishment, and we do so publicly and with emphasis, we are "singing" His praises. When our words convey a sincere feeling of elation at the overwhelming generosity of His blessings, we are praising God "for joy." And if the words we choose to give the honor of our accomplishment to the Lord are shared with as many other people as possible, then we have also praised Him "gloriously."

For example, say you're in a meeting of several people working as a team—the specific context does not matter—when the team's leader acknowledges a significant achievement of yours. You would be singing God's praises with joy and glory if you were to respond, smiling broadly, "Thank you so much, but I assure everyone that without the constant, powerful hand of the Lord on my shoulder all the way, I could never have achieved this. The glory here is His." Is this sort of thing easy? No way. Could it entail some risks? You bet. But let's not forget that another reason we praise God is for His constant renderings of justice in our lives. Take the risks, gentlemen—the Lord God will ensure a just result for you.

Several years ago, I was reporting to the executives of one of the nation's largest corporations, as in-house counsel for that company, about an important legal victory that had been obtained for the company by a team of attorneys whom I led in that process. When the highest-ranking officer in the room noted that I, in particular, should be thanked as the main person to acknowledge for the accomplishment, I somehow got up the courage (no doubt with the help of the Holy Spirit) to respond by telling everyone there, in a joyful, celebratory fashion, that I owed the success entirely to my Lord and Savior. The room fell silent, and the senior executive in question, without saying anything, merely gave me a disapproving look. However, less than five minutes after the meeting concluded, that executive stopped me in the hall and thanked me for giving my testimony. He said he had always wanted to do the same sort of thing within the company, but somehow he could never gather quite enough gumption to step outside his comfort zone in that manner. He said he felt that my spontaneous, bold confession of faith, in such a decidedly secular realm, had given him the motivation he needed to do likewise at his next opportunity.

Now, do you think I was feeling a bit apprehensive as this officer approached me briskly in the hallway right after this meeting? You know that I was. I was practically trembling as he strode toward me, imagining all sorts of chastisements that he could deliver to me for "evangelizing" in a corporate business meeting of senior executives. Yet, look how it all turned out: there was absolutely no call for my uneasiness. I should have remembered the Lord's divine pledge to dispense justice unfailingly among His people. That's what He did for me; that's what He'll do for you.

These verses provide us with a totally unambiguous example of how we praise our Savior. Please note the word: "*Save*-ior." That's what He did for every one of us, and our praise to Him in daily life is a pure recounting of what He has done for us. By grace, it is what we all are inclined to do. Now, for many of us, offering the type of public spiritual testimony described in my story is uncomfortable at best, and can entail risks—especially in the business context—that we often do not feel we can afford to take. I, however, would respectfully frame the issue differently: in light of what He has already done for us and His ever-faithful promise of justice, how can we keep from doing so?

Praise Him without restraint, because in Christ, He loves you without restraint.

....

Please note the word: "*Save*-ior." That's what He did for every one of us, and our praise to Him in daily life is a pure recounting of what He has done for us.

Prayer: Lord God, too often my lips are silent when it comes to praising You for all that You have done for me and for those I love. Cleanse my heart and my lips so that I might praise You rightly, so that others might praise You for eternity. I ask this through Christ, my Lord. Amen.

....

Monday

DAILY STUDY QUESTIONS
Psalm 66:1–4

1. When was the last time you shouted your joy over something that happened?

2. Why is such spontaneous expression of delight quite appropriate in our relationship with God?

3. Notice that the psalmist has high expectations for the sort of praise that should be given to God. How does "all the earth" shout for joy to God?

4. So great are God's power and actions that even those who oppose Him will be forced to admit His authority, though not happily. What's the difference between feigned obedience and obedience that is genuine?

5. How will you use your life to sing praises to God in the day ahead?

Psalm 66:5-7

>   Come and see what God has done: He is awesome in His
>   deeds toward the children of man. He turned the sea into dry
>   land; they passed through the river on foot. There did we re-
>   joice in Him, who rules by His might forever, whose eyes keep
>   watch on the nations—let not the rebellious exalt themselves.
>   *Selah*

Eyes Fully Open

Each of us can recall that crushing feeling that no matter *what* you do, you cannot possibly overcome the gigantic problem that life has placed squarely in your path. And you know what? You are right—you cannot. Without God, for example, Moses could have stood on the banks of the Red Sea and beat on it with his rod until all that remained were splinters. But not a drop of water would have been removed from the sea bed; the path of his people's salvation would have remained covered with water, and the Egyptians following in hot pursuit would have found easy prey. But God once again intervened to save His people from certain annihilation by parting the Red Sea just in time. In the same way, He chose to save us at just the right time by sending us Jesus, who through His obedient life and His own Baptism on the cross, reconciled us to God (Luke 12:50; Romans 5:9–11; Galatians 4:4–5). Through that singular act of supreme compassion, our Lord (a) saved us, and (b) enacted justice on our sinful nature and on Satan's dominion.

In verses 5–7, the psalmist clarifies once again why we joyfully praise our Lord and Savior. We know all about His earthly, historically accurate, magnificent acts of immense compassion and power, such as the Red Sea and Jordan crossings in the Old Testament. However, we mustn't lose sight of their deeper, spiritual significance. All such occurrences show that God saves. God saving the Hebrews through the Red Sea points forward to God saving us. In Romans 6, Paul teaches that God saved us through Jesus' Baptism on the cross (see Luke 12:50). He worked justice upon our old, corrupt, sinful nature and upon Satan's earthly dominion over us. Through our Baptism, God connects us to Jesus' Baptism, to which the Red Sea crossing points (see 1 Corinthians 10:1–2).

Do you not know that all of us who have been baptized into Christ Jesus were baptized into His death? We were buried therefore with Him by baptism into death, in order that, just as Christ was raised from the dead by the glory of the Father, we too might walk in newness of life. (Romans 6:3–4)

Years ago, I was in-house counsel for one of the largest and most powerful corporations in the nation. I had recently been promoted and relocated to Dallas when, out of the blue, my wife and I were invited to a holiday party for officers at the home of an officer. Wow! Little old me? Now, I had worked like a dog to earn this promotion, and I wasn't about to pass up a personal invitation to "soar with the eagles," even if only for one evening. I was determined to make a great impression and prove them right in granting me the very tangible recognition of a new title and a new paycheck in a great, new city.

While my wife and I were unfamiliar with Dallas's sprawling layout, we left our home in what we thought would be plenty of time. And although it was very slow going, at first it appeared that we would make it on time—barely. That's when it happened: as I hurriedly approached a major, Texas-sized intersection, I saw immediately that traffic was backed up nearly a *mile* in front of the traffic light. We were *so* close to our destination, but it was clear that the traffic light would surely render us inexcusably late for the party if we failed to get through ASAP.

After at least six repetitions of the light's infuriating pattern, we finally were only a few cars away from the football field-sized intersection. You probably know what happened next. The car directly in front of us moved at a speed indicating that the driver had no place to go and all the time in the world to get there. Despite my shouts of "encouragement" that he please let us both get through the green light, he made it through—but we did not. Drat! We were now unacceptably late. I was sure my career was over, and I even presumed to ask God aloud why He would do this to me. Well, His answer would come at the very next intersection.

After the stubborn traffic light turned green again, we proceeded to the next intersection, where we came upon the scene of a horrific automobile accident that had just happened. Someone coming from the right had violently "T-boned" the car that was heading in the same direction we were. We learned later that the offending driver had run a red light and the resulting collision killed everyone in the other car. As we drove cautiously around the wreckage, with emergency vehicles already screaming toward the intersection, I suddenly had an awful realization: the T-boned car *was the very car* that had gone so slowly in front of us and had kept us from proceeding through the traffic light! I had used foul language and deigned to challenge the Lord's judgment when, all along, God was working His compassion and justice.

Although He made us late, I believe He did so to save our lives, because had we made it through the preceding light along with the pokey car in front of us, our car could have been T-boned just a few hundred yards farther down the road. Although according to His mysterious will the Lord allowed the passengers in the other car to perish, He saved us from that accident. To top it all off, He made so many of the officers late—due to the same car accident—that no one noticed our untimely arrival.

Brothers in Christ, keep your eyes on the road and *fully open* all the time. Our unbelievably merciful and just God is lovingly watching over us and all people in all nations all of the time—even when it appears to us that just the opposite is happening. Trust in the Lord when He throws a tough road in front of you. Take a closer look and *you just may see* that the tough road is, in truth, an incredible blessing that just happens to be in the form of a most convincing disguise. "Come and *see* what God has done" (Psalm 66:5).

....

Brothers in Christ, keep your eyes on the road and *fully open* all the time. Our unbelievably merciful and just God is lovingly watching over us, and all people in all nations, all of the time.

Prayer: Heavenly Father, You keep watch on all the nations, and nothing occurs without Your watchful eye and Your providential care. Forgive me for second-guessing You, and help me to use my lips to bless, so that others might know of Your saving grace. In Jesus' name. Amen.

....

DAILY STUDY QUESTIONS
Psalm 66:5–7

1. How does the psalmist seem to support the old "Seeing is believing" adage?

2. Where would you take someone if you wanted to provide evidence of God's works on behalf of man—that is, you?

3. Have you ever experienced a "close call" that convinced you of God's explicit and protecting intervention in the course of life? How does recognition of such interventions have everything to do with one's way of seeing—that is, one's presuppositions about—life?

4. What is the not-so-thinly veiled threat of verse 7?

5. What works do you expect God to perform on your behalf today? Does your answer reflect the view of the psalmist or the view of a skeptic?

Psalm 66:8–12

> Bless our God, O peoples; let the sound of His praise be heard, who has kept our soul among the living and has not let our feet slip. For You, O God, have tested us; You have tried us as silver is tried. You brought us into the net; You laid a crushing burden on our backs; You let men ride over our heads; we went through fire and through water; yet You have brought us out to a place of abundance.

Out on a . . . Root

Have you ever been directly confronted by a sudden, life-threatening event? If this has happened to you on more than one occasion (say, for example, you are a combat veteran), can you remember the first time it ever happened to you? I do. It was a long, long time ago, when I was only seven or eight years old. Back then, I didn't know anything about Psalm 66:8–12. But now, I'm living proof of the truth and power reflected in these verses.

In our earthly times of great distress, we do well to remember not only these verses from the psalmist, but also the directly related and critically important teaching from Paul's pen, that "for those who love God all things work together for good, for those who are called according to His purpose" (Romans 8:28; see also Philippians 2:13). Now, I don't know about you, but personally, when I have just lived through a devastating personal disaster, I always have a bit of difficulty recalling Scripture's promise to believers that God will ensure something good comes from even horrible situations. Perhaps you've had a similar experience. But I am so confident in the truth that pours out of these two passages that I am quite willing to make this promise: gentlemen, if you are indeed called according to His purpose, and if only you take the time for quiet prayer and clear thought in the wake of a personal devastation, no matter how severe, you will see, in time, that very good things ultimately flow from the event that caused such great harm in your life. Sound like I'm "going out on a limb"? Yes. But I've been there before; read on.

Everyone has a Danny Mertz in his life as a kid. Danny lived across the street from me in South Omaha, when I was about eight and he was about ten. We lived less than a block away from 20th Street, a very busy four-lane thoroughfare at the top of our hill. At that time, ours was a poor-but-proud Slavic neighborhood, blessed with some very good people (except for Danny). Now, my mother had warned me to stay away from the Mertz boy, and she had *severely* warned me to stay away from 20th Street; I was not to even *think* about trying to cross it to get to the cool little public park directly on the other side from our street. But, alas, under the awesome peer pressure of a big, ornery neighborhood bully like Danny "The Destroyer" Mertz, I was putty in his hands.

Once we got across the street, he goaded me across a large, open field to a point on a small cliff overlooking the Platte River. There, he showed me a "really cool" way to get down on my stomach and hang down off of the cliff. Then, by grabbing onto the grass, I could slowly lower myself down to the mouth of a big cave, until I could rest my feet on an exposed tree root that was suspended across the opening of the cave. Danny proceeded to do this with ease and then assured me that if I didn't do likewise, I surely lacked certain important parts of the male anatomy. If he can do it, I can do it, I thought, but I forgot that he was two years older and six inches taller than I was.

As I dangled there in midair, trying desperately to hang on to my two fistfuls of slippery grass, unable to feel my way down to the safety of the tree root below my feet, screaming for help, and watching Danny run away, I remembered only too clearly my mother's stern warning and specific orders. I was actually more worried about facing her wrath than I was about letting go and tumbling down fifty feet of sheer rock face all the way to—and probably under—the river roaring below. But I had experienced two years of Catholic grade school at that point and so I knew how to pray—and pray I did. Hard. The grass in my grasp was now ripping out of the ground, and I slowly slid downward toward certain death. My eyes were squeezed shut and I prayed out loud (it was impossible to look down for the tree root) as my feet frantically searched for the life-saving root. As I slipped down farther and farther without feeling anything catch on the bottoms of my sneakers, I truly thought these were my last seconds on earth. But eventually, even my short legs reached the tree root, and the Lord placed the bottoms of my shoes directly over it until my perilous descent suddenly stopped. I carefully tight-roped across the root to one side of the cave entrance, then climbed gingerly down the rest of the cliff and walked home on wobbly, trembling legs.

You want to talk about being "tested" and "tried"? I don't think I ever did another single thing wrong the remainder of my kid life. The Lord kept my feet from slipping that day, and at the same time gave me such a serious lesson in obedience that I did in fact come out the other side in sterling form, at least as far as adhering to my parents' rules was concerned. But let's all please be certain we don't miss the real point here: again, the psalmist has been inspired by God to write a psalm that conveys his experience and God's people's experience real-time. But there's more. It's about testing and trying us as He conforms us to the image of His Son (Romans 8:29).

And so, my brothers in Christ, let us give thanks and praise every day of our lives for being blessed to be among those who are "called according to His purpose." It is because we are so called that we have the desire and the ability to make it through those supremely trying times in earthly life and come out on the other side of them purified. And know that our spiritual "place of abundance" puts to shame any man's image of the "land of milk and honey," for our place is in the glorious, loving presence of our Lord and Savior, Jesus Christ, for the rest of eternity. Being left "hanging" for the comparatively short period of our earthly lives, even with all of life's potential trials and tribulations, is small in comparison to eternity!

....

And so, my brothers in Christ, let us give thanks and praise every day of our lives for being blessed to be among those who are "called according to His purpose."

Prayer: Dear Holy Spirit, during my times of hardship or testing, keep my mind and heart focused on God's rich promises to me in Christ. Cause His Word to dwell in me richly, even as I look to the abundant life of the world to come. I ask this in Jesus' name. Amen.

....

Wednesday

DAILY STUDY QUESTIONS
Psalm 66:8-12

1. When have you experienced a time, in childhood or more recently, when life seemed to hang in the balance?

2. Did you learn anything from that event at the time? What can you learn from it now?

3. How does the psalmist view the affliction that he is enduring? What is its source and meaning?

4. When do you expect God to do for you what He did for His people, Israel, and bring you into "a place of abundance"?

5. What things are happening in your life today that would look quite different if you learned to see them as tools that God is using to refine you?

Psalm 66:13–15

> I will come into Your house with burnt offerings; I will per-
> form my vows to You, that which my lips uttered and my mouth
> promised when I was in trouble. I will offer to You burnt of-
> ferings of fattened animals, with the smoke of the sacrifice of
> rams; I will make an offering of bulls and goats. *Selah*

Vows and Promises

Psalm 66 has reminded us this week of God's incredible faithfulness to us. Because of His faithfulness, we who are "called according to His purpose" (Romans 8:28) strive to fulfill our vows made to Him. Now, we all *try* to do this, right? However, if you are one who has, on occasion, failed to meet some promise you had made to the Lord, please raise your hand. Okay, you can regrasp the book with both hands now, as will I. We all knew how that one would come out. We know how easy it is to make promises to the Lord when we're in some kind of trouble, and how easy it is to forget them once He has again rescued us from our woes.

But men, have you ever stopped to realize that promises made *to other people—* family members, friends, employers, and so on—also constitute promises "made to God"? As you bear in mind the words of verses 13–15 and read on, please also recall these words of Jesus: "As you did it to one of the least of these My brothers, you did it to Me" (Matthew 25:40). Clearly, Jesus is saying that our actions toward all of our brothers and sisters in faith are actions toward Him.

Consider the promises we make in marriage. Now, it is not the purpose of this chapter to discuss in depth the many important things God has said about marriage. Suffice it to say that contemporary views of this sacred institution are no doubt woefully off the mark in God's eyes. And apart from marriage, it is difficult to imagine a better example of a righteous promise to another person that should be viewed as a promise made directly to the Lord. For now, I will say only that all of us men would do well to reread the many helpful Scripture passages on this subject, and to rededicate ourselves to our wives, our marriages, and, therefore, our God.

But what about other promises we make to other people? What about everyday promises made to those around us at home, in the workplace, or in our community of friends? Clearly, the Bible commands that we consider all such promises as vows made directly to the Lord! I don't know about you, but this truth gives me pause. Guys, I would venture to guess that I'm not the only one among our number who sometimes forgets that God views our promises to others as promises to Him. A great friend from my past—let's call him "Lynn"—emphasized this important point to me many years ago, in a situation that I believe nearly everyone would categorize as quite a surprise.

Lynn had been a work colleague and was a very close friend from many years earlier. I had been transferred away from our hometown of St. Louis, but his lot at that time was to remain. When I joyously told him some months later that I was to be married in my new home of San Antonio, Lynn promised to be present for this important day of my life. What Lynn didn't know at the time was that during the period between his promise and my wedding, his teenage son, his soccer-star son, would be involved in a tragic car accident that would take one of his legs from the knee down.

Needless to say, during those first few months after the horrible accident, Lynn and I spent a great deal of time on the phone. Clearly, he was severely challenged by the many parental duties and tasks that he owed his son. He spent every single day in the hospital with the boy, lifting, mentoring, cheerleading, witnessing. Lynn was constantly challenged just to keep his boy from becoming hopelessly suicidal. Of course, I never mentioned my upcoming wedding during this awful period of my friend's life. Certainly there was no way Lynn could get away from his immediate family and his obligations there just to go to a workmate's wedding in a city nine hundred miles away.

Nevertheless, when I went to answer the front door in my crisp, new wedding tux and mirrorlike shoes, there was Lynn, his right hand extended to me for a shake. He was standing on my front porch, a beautifully wrapped gift under his left arm and an even more beautiful smile on his face. I was, of course, speechless. When he finally asked if the wedding was indoors or outdoors, I snapped out of my shock and warmly ushered him inside.

After the ceremony, as the evening wore on, I learned more and more about what it means to be a true Christian from my great friend, Lynn. To him, that little promise he had made to me was just as important as any promise he ever made directly to his Lord and Savior. I expressed amazement that he could justify leaving the very sensitive and dangerous situation with his son just to be with me for the modest ceremony in my home so far from his. All he would say in response was that he was absolutely certain God would protect his boy while he took the time to honor a righteous promise made to a brother. And he said this without so much as a quiver in his voice or a blink of his eyes.

And he was right. Upon his return to St. Louis, Lynn found that his son had made sudden, remarkable progress during the two days Lynn was away. He later had several surgeries, and, wearing a carefully made prosthetic device, he ultimately flourished to the point that he played in goal during the final game of his high school's postseason tournament, to the amazement of all in attendance—except me. By that point, I knew that our God is unfailingly faithful to us, and that all He asks in return is that we love Him and one another.

Psalm 66 is an excellent reminder to all of us to take very, very seriously all vows we make to all people. Keeping our word is part of our reasonable sacrifice—not of fattened animals or rams, but of hearts, minds, and lips cleansed by the forgiving blood of Christ. Be true to your word to everyone, gentlemen. Be a Lynn for someone as soon as you can. Because when you do, you point others to Christ, who never breaks His promises and keeps every single one of them in His Word.

....

Keeping our word is part of our reasonable sacrifice—not of fattened animals or rams, but of hearts, minds, and lips cleansed by the forgiving blood of Christ.

Prayer: Dear God, Your Word is truth, and Your Son is Truth in human flesh. By the power of Your Spirit, forgive me for the times I have not kept my promises, and enable me to be a man of my word, a man of Your Word, so that others might know of Your faithfulness. I ask this in Jesus' name. Amen.

....

Thursday

DAILY STUDY QUESTIONS
Psalm 66:13–15

1. What's the most significant vow that you have made in the past year or so?

2. How might (or how *did*) the point of the devotion alter your last answer?

3. In a time of distress or great fear, have you ever made a "bargain" with God? How did it turn out? Would you do it again?

4. Notice the psalmist's description of the temple in verse 13. How might using this name for your place of worship affect the way you approach your participation in the Divine Service?

5. The author of our text paid his vow with rams, bulls, and goats. How will you pay your vows today?

Psalm 66:16-20

> Come and hear, all you who fear God, and I will tell what
> He has done for my soul. I cried to Him with my mouth, and
> high praise was on my tongue. If I had cherished iniquity in
> my heart, the Lord would not have listened. But truly God has
> listened; He has attended to the voice of my prayer. Blessed
> be God, because He has not rejected my prayer or removed His
> steadfast love from me!

The Lord Saves

When was the last time God saved your life? Hard to remember? That's okay. He knows we humans can't even perceive—much less recall—every time He saves us. *But* that does not stop Him from doing so more often than we'll ever know during our earthly life. In verses 16–20, the psalmist tells everyone all of the wonderful things God had done for him, especially by hearing and answering the psalmist's prayer. We would all be lost—in this life and the next—without God's infinite and constant mercy and love! Those of us who are blessed to be "called according to His purpose" (Romans 8:28) know what the Lord Jesus has done for us eternally, dying on the cross for the forgiveness of sins we could never redress on our own. But do we really perceive and acknowledge all that He does for us temporally, every day?

Importantly, the psalmist notes in verse 18 that had he held sin in his heart as he prayed to God, the Lord would not have listened. This is a critical passage, men. We can't expect God to bless us or our undertakings when we knowingly and persistently refuse to repent. We can't "cry" to Him and "praise" Him when we "cherish" sin. Here John makes clear both the deception of sinlessness this side of heaven and the cleansing confession of truth:

> If we say we have no sin, we deceive ourselves, and the
> truth is not in us. If we confess our sins, He is faithful and just
> to forgive us our sins and to cleanse us from all unrighteous-
> ness. (1 John 1:8-9)

We learned this week that by loving others, we love the Lord, and by doing right by others, we do right by the Lord. God promises His mercy and blessings when we seek to serve Him. Then why do we all find it so very difficult to do this? I don't purport to know all of the reasons, but I would humbly offer one for consideration: in my case, anyway, I know that all too often, I fail to see the connection between my acts of love for the Lord and His loving provision in all things as I seek to serve Him.

A few years ago, my wife and I decided to take the leap and build our retirement "dream home." Now, we had both been blessed with wonderful careers, so this was to be a considerable home and a considerable investment. In other words, credit-wise, once approved, we were *really* hanging out on this one! Satan is always busy in the lives of believers, and this was no exception.

And then, shortly after we entered into this substantial financial commitment, my wife suddenly and unexpectedly lost her job. Not long thereafter, and also before we would have to requalify for our loan amount to meet closing requirements, I lost one of my sources of income without warning. I still had a modest pension, but the payout from my main source of retirement income, a deferred-compensation plan, would not begin for another year and a half. To make matters worse, we both still were trying to sell our other homes from before our marriage, at least one of which absolutely had to sell before we could close on our new home—and there were no interested parties in sight. The combination of all these factors made it clear that unless something changed, we definitely would not requalify for financing in time to close on our new home, and we would lose any opportunity to own such a home.

One Saturday during this bleak period in our relationship, we were going over the budget, trying to find things to cut. Tithing at church came up for discussion. I'm embarrassed to say that my maleness overcame my Christianity for a moment, and in the typical, dominant, protective mode of thinking, I suggested that it would help if we suspended our tithing at least until we could get back on our feet. To her infinite credit, my wonderful wife would have nothing of it. She reminded me that we are commanded to trust in the Lord in all things and lay all our earthly troubles at His feet. "But what are we going to *do?*" I implored. "Tithe and pray," she replied. We prayed on this, together, every night at bedtime.

I promise you this is all true: The next day, Sunday, we continued to tithe as we had been doing. During the following week, (a) I sold my home; (b) my wife got a fine offer on her home; and (c) I was assigned a huge case by the Atlanta law firm for which I had been working on a minimal, ad hoc, "of counsel" basis before that time. The offer on my wife's home eventually turned into a final sale—and in plenty of time to close on our new home—and my big case turned into thousands of dollars in billed hours of legal work—also in time to seal our loan requalification for closing on our new home. Now, this is no claim that such a turnaround in events will happen for everyone finding themselves in a similar situation. I am just saying that it happened to us, and we give God all the credit.

As the psalmist reminds us, when we pray to God in repentant faith, He will listen to our prayers and respond with mercy and love as only He can. Because our great High Priest, Jesus Christ, was "tempted as we are, yet without sin. . . . [We can] with confidence draw near to the throne of grace, that we may receive mercy and find grace to help in time of need" (Hebrews 4:15–16). Confident in God's mercy and forgiveness in our Savior, we can begin to look more closely at all the different ways that the Lord saves us in our temporal lives. God is faithful in His promises; He hears and answers our prayers according to His gracious will, and His steadfast love remains forever. Blessed be God!

....

As the psalmist reminds us, when we pray to God in repentant faith, He will listen to our prayers and respond with mercy and love as only He can. . . . "[We can] with confidence draw near to the throne of grace, that we may receive mercy and find grace to help in time of need" (Hebrews 4:15–16).

Prayer: Lord Jesus Christ, our great High Priest, You have opened heaven for us through Your broken body and poured-out blood. Cleanse me from all sin, and hear and answer my prayer in accordance with God's gracious will. I ask this in Your name. Amen.

....

DAILY STUDY QUESTIONS
Psalm 66:16–20

1. Think for a minute or two about all that God has done for you so far this one day. Why, do you think, are we humans so prone to forget the reality of God's giving?

2. In verse 16, whom does the psalmist invite to hear his story of the Lord's provision? What can this teach you about your responsibility toward other believers?

3. It seems that when he was pleading for God's mercy, the author of this psalm prayed *two* things (v. 17). What does this teach you about the content of your praying—even in dire straits?

4. The psalmist is aware of an absolute "deal breaker," or, more accurately, "relationship breaker" (v. 18). If sin blocks prayer and destroys one's relationship with God, then what hope is there for people who are, by definition, always sinners?

5. Answered prayer is wonderful; an unbroken relationship with God is even better (v. 20). When your prayers are not receiving yes for an answer, what assurance do you have of God's favor?

Week Two

Psalm 66

The 66th psalm is a psalm of thanks for the general blessing that God often delivers and protects His people out of the hand of the enemies, as He did at the Red Sea. The histories in the books of the Judges and Kings are full of these deliverances, which He also does daily for us, delivering and keeping His own in the true faith against the devil, spirits, and sins.

—Martin Luther

GROUP BIBLE STUDY
(Questions and answers on pp. 190–193.)

1. Can you recall a time when you experienced such a remarkable blessing or received such good news that you could not help telling even strangers what had happened? Tell the group about it.

2. Since the whole earth is invited (commanded!?) to give praise to God (vv. 1, 4), in what ways can a man seek to join his voice with a creationwide symphony rather than merely offer his own individual ditties?

3. How can you tell when someone comes cringing to God (v. 3)? What difference does it make?

4. The psalm celebrates God's mercy displayed in the dry water crossings of the exodus. What good does it do us to remember such ancient events? What is the purpose of these divine interventions?

5. What kind of watch does God keep on the nations? How do you reconcile the reality of enormous evil at work in so many nations with a God who keeps watch?

6. Does the confident promise of verse 12 (and even the wonderful assurance of Romans 8:28) mean that we will always see good things happen if we simply continue to wait patiently and faithfully? How might it be possible for such thinking to become problematic or even dangerous?

7. What abrupt shift does the psalm makes at verse 13? (Pay attention to the first-person pronouns.) What do you think of this move? How does this shift shed light on the relationship between the individual and the congregation?

8. Considering Jesus' stern counsel in Matthew 5:36–37, what's the difference between taking a vow, making a promise, agreeing to something, and merely giving tacit assent?

9. Some would like to summarize the Christian faith with a handful of basic principles that, when kept, guarantee God's blessings: love God, love people, get blessed. Do you think this is what the psalmist meant in the last verses of this psalm? What's the problem with this sort of thinking? What would you say to someone who was promoting it?

10. What vows need your renewed attention? What testimony do you need to give to fellow believers? What praise do you need to include in your routine petitions? In other words, what difference will this psalm and its message make in the way that you live in the days to come?

Week Three

Psalm 116

[1] I love the LORD, because He has heard
my voice and my pleas for mercy.

[2] Because He inclined His ear to me,
therefore I will call on Him as long as I live.

[3] The snares of death encompassed me;
the pangs of Sheol laid hold on me;
I suffered distress and anguish.

[4] Then I called on the name of the LORD:
"O LORD, I pray, deliver my soul!"

[5] Gracious is the LORD, and righteous;
our God is merciful.

[6] The LORD preserves the simple;
when I was brought low, He saved me.

[7] Return, O my soul, to your rest;
for the LORD has dealt bountifully with you.

[8] For You have delivered my soul from death,
my eyes from tears,
my feet from stumbling;

[9] I will walk before the LORD
in the land of the living.

[10] I believed, even when I spoke,
"I am greatly afflicted";

[11] I said in my alarm,
"All mankind are liars."

¹² What shall I render to the LORD
for all His benefits to me?

¹³ I will lift up the cup of salvation
and call on the name of the LORD,

¹⁴ I will pay my vows to the LORD
in the presence of all His people.

¹⁵ Precious in the sight of the LORD
is the death of His saints.

¹⁶ O LORD, I am Your servant;
I am Your servant, the son of Your maidservant.
You have loosed my bonds.

¹⁷ I will offer to You the sacrifice of thanksgiving
and call on the name of the LORD.

¹⁸ I will pay my vows to the LORD
in the presence of all His people,

¹⁹ in the courts of the house of the LORD,
in your midst, O Jerusalem.
Praise the LORD!

Mike Furrey

Psalm 116:1–4

> I love the LORD, because He has heard my voice and my pleas for mercy. Because He inclined His ear to me, therefore I will call on Him as long as I live. The snares of death encompassed me; the pangs of Sheol laid hold on me; I suffered distress and anguish. Then I called on the name of the LORD: "O LORD, I pray, deliver my soul!"

The Lord Delivers

Because the world we live in is filled with anger, disappointment, and fear, some people try to ease their pain inappropriately with drugs, alcohol, or sexual sins. Although God gives us all that we need for this life, we are seldom satisfied with His blessings—we yearn for more. Decisions we make during the day disturb our sleep at night. We never love our neighbors as much as we love ourselves. Presuming to be supermen, we walk around with S's on our chests while all sorts of "baggage" hangs from our backs. We look not to the Scriptures, but to newspapers, magazines, and the Internet for answers. We allow our jobs to affect the way we treat our kids. We never end up truly honoring our mother and father. We celebrate Jesus only twice a year, at Easter and Christmas, even though He saved us from an eternal death.

The first four verses of Psalm 116 don't paint a pretty picture, do they? The psalmist is not in a good place. He feels like death and hell are surrounding him. And yet, he still cries out to the Lord for help.

I have often pondered the idea of dying. What will dying be like? Who will be the first person I see when I get to heaven? When I was a young boy, I was scared of dying. During the day, my head was filled with ideas and thoughts typical for a boy my age. But at night, I was haunted by the idea that heaven might not exist. I had trouble dealing with the thought that my life might be pointless. The hard work, the dedication, the determination—all these things that I valued and that were instilled in me as a boy would count for nothing. To be honest, I have to admit that I wasn't so much scared of death; I was *angry*.

We all face those moments. The psalmist certainly did. They are called "ups and downs," wins and losses, good days and bad. A lot of times we barely avoid ruining our lives by making a correct last-minute decision that spares us from a lifetime of regret. Some people face those moments but make the *wrong* decision, and then end up growing old behind bars. We humans don't fully grasp the idea that Satan really is out to get us, especially we who are of the household of faith. The devil takes the frustrations and anxiety we experience during our daily grind and manipulates them to his own wicked ends. Life challenges us to see if we will break, and when we do, more often than not we blame not ourselves but the people around us—our wives, our kids, our friends. Then, angry and unable to flee the situation, we pick a fight, even with God Himself.

As I said, I have struggled with the idea of death my whole life. Even though I go to church and believe in God and in heaven, I still struggle with it. Every time I get in an airplane, I start to worry. I travel quite a bit, and I still haven't gotten used to the turbulence. I never could figure out how a mass of metal can become airborne. I also would rather be behind the wheel than in the passenger seat. Any time our boundaries are threatened, or if we lose control over any part of our lives, we become fearful. Every morning we wake up with the desire to accomplish our goals for the day. However, if we don't get that important phone call on time, if we fail to catch the bus, or if something else goes wrong, our day is "completely ruined." But is it—*really*? Even we Christians put so much pressure on ourselves and on others—at our job with our colleagues, at home with our wife and kids, even out with our friends—that we end up damaging important relationships, all because *we* can't handle *not* being in control.

Here, Jesus puts our anxiety in perspective. He says,

> "Therefore I tell you, do not be anxious about your life, what you will eat or what you will drink, nor about your body, what you will put on. Is not life more than food, and the body more than clothing?" (Matthew 6:25)

Jesus is not telling us to avoid schedules or to miss appointments. Rather, He is inviting us to keep things in perspective—His perspective. *God* is in control. He knows about our needs even before we know about them, and He will provide all that we require. God is *still* in control, even when it appears that our lives, our days, or our schedules are out of control. Paul says, "If you confess with your mouth that Jesus is Lord and believe in your heart that God raised Him from the dead, you will be saved" (Romans 10:9). So even though we are encompassed by the "snares of death" or "the pangs of Sheol," in Christ we are still saved! Dead to this world and alive in Christ, I am set free from fearing airplanes, car rides, and tough decisions. I am at peace falling asleep at night, and I awake with joy. I am honored to be a loving husband to my wife and a loving father to my children. More than anything, though, I am glad I that I have a Friend who listens to every thought and prayer.

God invites us to trust in Him because He will deliver. Every morning, give thanks to Him for waking you up and for giving you another day. Every night before you go to sleep, put your body and soul into His hands. He will always "deliver us from evil," and He will never leave us. Let your heart be filled with Christ, because He has set you free from sins, from death, from Satan's control, from anxiety, and from the anger that results from loss of control. Wherever you are, whatever situation you are in, the Lord will deliver you. Jesus is with you all the time, hearing you when you pray, and present with you in His name. Look to Him, "the founder and perfecter of our faith" (Hebrew 12:2).

God invites us to trust in Him because He will deliver. Every morning, give thanks to Him for waking you up and for giving you another day. Every night before you go to sleep, put your body and soul into His hands.

Prayer: Dear God, You hear my prayers and answer them for the sake of Christ and according to Your gracious will. Because He conquered sin, death, and the devil for me on the cross, set me free from my fears and anxieties so that I may serve You and Your people. In Jesus' name. Amen.

DAILY STUDY QUESTIONS
Psalm 116:1–4

1. What's the closest you have ever come to death? How did the experience change you?

2. How do you understand the first verse of the psalm? Is the psalmist suggesting a conditional love of God—that he only loves the Lord because he has been given what he sought?

3. What do the references to "snares of death" and "pangs of Sheol" convey about the psalmist's experience with death (v. 3)? How does this agree or disagree with your own experience?

4. What makes verse 4 the ideal model for our own dealings with the terrors of death?

5. Based on the example of the psalmist's prayer, do your own prayers tend to be too verbose or too simplistic?

Psalm 116:5–7

> Gracious is the LORD, and righteous; our God is merciful. The LORD preserves the simple; when I was brought low, He saved me. Return, O my soul, to your rest; for the LORD has dealt bountifully with you.

Counting Stars, Not Sheep

Verses 5–7 of our psalm contrast the grace, righteousness, and mercy of the Lord with our simplicity and need. In a sense, the psalmist is presenting the gracious love of our heavenly Father and our great need as His children.

What do you remember about your childhood? During the day, children experience a lot of joy as they play with friends on the playground. In fact, how often do you see at kid alone at the playground? They are often joyfully jumping, swinging, or playing with a companion. On the playground, kids can meet and make new friends, some of whom may influence their lives in one way or another. Then again, at nighttime, children sometimes experience a lot of fear, particularly the fear of being alone or the fear of the dark. Being alone and in the dark can be scary for a child. Every creak in the floor, rafters, or walls, every strong gust of wind outside, can be scary. Kids sometimes fear that a stranger might be in the house, even though the doors and windows are locked and the house is completely quiet. When a child feels alone or afraid, the comforting words and touch of his or her mother, father, or grandparent can calm and soothe the soul. All grown up, we adults still need mercy from our heavenly Father, as well as from our family members and friends.

I still remember the first day that we moved into a new house. I was so excited that I would get my own room and wouldn't have to bunk with my older brother anymore. Having a room of my own meant that I could hang my sports posters wherever I wanted. I could pick the place for my bed. I spent that whole day in my room, decorating every wall and sweeping out every corner. Needless to say, it was spotless. Because it was a Sunday night and school started the next day, we had to go to bed early. I was excited about school, about my room, and about my life. When I put my head down on the pillow, it was still daylight. I tried lying on my side, then my back, trying to figure out which position gave me the best view of my new room. Gradually my room grew darker and darker until it was pitch black, with only a moonbeam shining through the window and onto the floor. Now the excitement of the day began to fade, and I began to think more and more about school. I became anxious, which caused me to toss and turn.

While I could no longer see objects inside my bedroom, the door was open, and I could make out the steps to the second floor. As I lay there, I imagined that someone might be peeping around the corner as they came up the stairs. I guess you could say that my awesome new bedroom turned into fear in a box! At first, I was so happy to have a room of my own; but when it became so dark and quiet, I wanted my brother back so that I had someone to talk to. I wanted to turn the light on to give me peace of mind. After that first night, I wanted to give my new bedroom back.

Being that young, I didn't understand how your mind sometimes plays tricks on you. I didn't know then that the best time for the devil to attack is when you are alone. I have learned that about the prince of darkness over the years. That first night in my new room was the only night I was so uncomfortable, but afterward, I sometimes wondered, where was God that night? Why didn't He just come and make everything better? At other times during my faith journey, I have sometimes wondered if God were sleeping! I know now what I didn't know then: God was with me all the time. Listen to God's encouragement of Joshua: "Have I not commanded you? Be strong and courageous. Do not be frightened, and do not be dismayed, for the LORD your God is with you wherever you go" (Joshua 1:9). Now listen to the Lord's encouragement to the disciples: "And behold, I am with you always, to the end of the age" (Matthew 28:20).

Some people think that God comes and goes, that He is with us only when we need Him or expect Him to help. The same people often crucify Him when He doesn't fix a problem or give a solution to their liking. The Bible tells us that no matter the circumstance, God is there. He might not give us all that we want. But hasn't He already given us what we need?

At night, when you lie alone or with your wife in bed, you are not alone. God the Holy Spirit dwells within you. Jesus never leaves your side, and when you fall asleep, you are at peace in His hands. Your best Friend, the One who listens to everything you say and cares about you, is with you always. No matter what your circumstances, God and His Word are your guide. He will comfort you in every decision you must make. He will illumine your way. Even though you may be weak, in Him you are strong. You may be simple, but He teaches you His ways. In the lowliness of your humanity, He saves you. In Christ, He gives your soul the rest you need. We should always count the stars, as Abraham did, and never worry about counting the sheep.

....

At night, when you lie alone or with your wife in bed, you are not alone. God the Holy Spirit dwells within you. Jesus never leaves your side, and when you fall asleep, you are at peace in His hands.

Prayer: Blessed Holy Spirit, I am a simple man. Teach me through Your Word. Through the mercy and merits of Christ, restore peace and joy in my heart, so that I might rest both my body and soul in the gracious hands of my Savior. In Jesus' name. Amen.

....

DAILY STUDY QUESTIONS
Psalm 116:5–7

1. When you were a child, what fears seemed to catch up with you each night as you waited for sleep to find you? What fears haunt those quiet moments these days?

2. What evidences of God's compassion have you recently experienced?

3. What do you think of when you hear that God "preserves the simple" (v. 6).? How does God preserve *your* life?

4. According to verse 7, what should be the normal state or status quo of a person's heart or soul? Why is this important?

5. What does the word *bountiful* imply? How is it a good descriptor of God's dealings with you?

Psalm 116:8–14

> For You have delivered my soul from death, my eyes from tears, my feet from stumbling; I will walk before the LORD in the land of the living. I believed, even when I spoke, "I am greatly afflicted"; I said in my alarm, "All mankind are liars." What shall I render to the LORD for all His benefits to me? I will lift up the cup of salvation and call on the name of the LORD, I will pay my vows to the LORD in the presence of all His people.

Lift Up the Cup

Today the psalmist asks, "What shall I render to the LORD for all His benefits to me?" Think about all God has given us. God is the Creator of this earth and everything in it. He took six days to create our universe, then rested on the seventh day. Perhaps God was so into the beautiful art He had created in nature that He rested to enjoy it! He has given us life; He has also given us parents, brothers, sisters, kids, and friends. He designed our world so that we can have everything we need to survive. Even after mankind's fall into sin, He revealed Himself and His plan of salvation, first to Adam and Eve, and then to prophets and authors of Scripture, giving them more and more information about a more perfect future through the coming Messiah, Jesus of Nazareth.

God reveals His divine nature and His creative power in creation. He is the teacher of all scientists. He hangs two symbols in the sky to light the days and the nights. Even more, He is so gracious that His Holy Spirit gives us faith through the Gospel of Jesus Christ so that, believing, we are healed from our sin. He hears everything we talk about, sees everything we see, and knows all of our problems. God is understanding and compassionate to all who follow Him. God fills our hearts with joy and love. God looks at all of us as His children and always comforts us. He is a God who "so loved the world, that He gave His only Son, that whoever believes in Him should not perish but have eternal life" (John 3:16). Can you think of any more of God's benefits? I know I can.

If we all were to look back in our lives, we would have to be thankful for what God has given us. It doesn't matter if you receive a salary or an hourly wage or if you have no job at all. All of us have been blessed. It's amazing to think that we humans are always looking to better ourselves. I have to admit that I have tried to do so a thousand times. It's true that we are born that way—our sinful human nature is never satisfied. Each of us has this character flaw, even if we have learned to control it. Everyone loves the promotion or raise. We love to hear the cheers and be honored for what we have accomplished. We are given titles as presidents, vice presidents, and so one. We wear nametags and badges that tell people who we are and our level of professional achievement. We take credit for the good we don't do and not enough credit for the bad we do. We concentrate more on the benefits we make for ourselves, rather than the benefits God gives us freely out of His fatherly hand.

My brother was one of the best baseball players in Ohio. As a kid, I always thought that if I could be like my brother, I could achieve anything. So I went to work, trying to accomplish that goal. I say this in humility, but I surpassed his accomplishments. I earned everything he did and more. I reached a higher plateau than he did. Sometimes people ask me if I am grateful for my brother. They reason that if it weren't for him, I wouldn't have accomplished what I have. Trust me, I am truly honored to have him as my brother, but did he really push me to the limit? Did my brother instill in me the passion to work? The honest truth is, no, he didn't. He supported me in everything I did, but he didn't give me the ability to do it all. He didn't create me to be who I have become. I love my brother, but it is God who has created us as unique human beings, each with his or her own special set of gifts.

For my part, among the many benefits God has given me is my family. I have been blessed with an amazing wife and three kids. Whom am I supposed to thank for that? Off the top of my head, I could list parents, teachers, and friends. Certainly they played a role. But God created each member of my family. He created the love and admiration I have for my wife and her love for me. Moses writes in Genesis 2:18, "Then the LORD God said, 'It is not good that the man should be alone; I will make him a helper fit for him.'" God is the one that brought Eve to Adam; He's the one that instituted the benefits of marriage and family.

While it is awesome to receive God's blessings, it is also important to receive those blessings with thanksgiving. The best way to give thanks to God, in my opinion, is the same way that you ask God for help. Just as you fall on your knees and have an intimate conversation with God, asking Him to heal the sick, save the relationship, or deliver you from disaster, you likewise fall to your knees in this moment of spiritual intimacy and offer humble thanks. Just as you seek help from God when you have a problem, you seek to give Him praise for the many benefits with which He has already blessed you.

No matter what happens in our daily lives, God reminds us of His presence and His promises. In nature, He has given us the rainbow to remind us of His promise never again to destroy the earth with a flood. In the rising of the sun and in the rain that falls upon the ground, He reminds us of His gracious provision. Indeed, as David says, "The heavens declare the glory of God, and the sky above proclaims His handiwork" (Psalm 19:1). Even more, God's Word reminds us of the salvation that He has freely accomplished for us in Christ. That's why, despite our titles, accomplishments, or whatever is written on our nametags and badges, we can lift up "the cup of salvation." Because Jesus is our Savior, we can call upon God in thankfulness for what He has done for us in His Son.

....

Just as you fall on your knees and have an intimate conversation with God, asking Him to heal the sick, save the relationship, or deliver you from disaster, you likewise fall to your knees in this moment of spiritual intimacy and offer humble thanks.

Prayer: Dear Jesus, You drank the bitter cup of sin and death on the cross so that I may drink Your cup of forgiveness and eternal life. Open my eyes to the many benefits You daily shower upon me, especially my family, friends, co-workers, and neighbors, so that I may give You thanks. In Your name I pray. Amen.

....

DAILY STUDY QUESTIONS
Psalm 116:8-14

1. How do you sort out the interface between your personal accomplishment and God's work through you?

2. Is verse 9 the response of the psalmist for what God has worked for him, or is it a declaration about the end result of God's work of saving?

3. How does "walking before the LORD" convey both an expectation and an encouragement? Which do you feel most of the time?

4. What important lesson about the Christian life does the first few words of verse 10 teach us?

5. What difference would it make in your own life if verse 12 were treated as more than merely rhetorical? What would happen if you earnestly asked yourself this question several times a day for the rest of this week?

Psalm 116:15–16

> Precious in the sight of the LORD is the death of His saints.
> O LORD, I am Your servant; I am Your servant, the son of Your
> maidservant. You have loosed my bonds.

Precious in God's Sight

Some people struggle with finding their purpose in life. Others struggle in their faith, while still others find it hard to find peace in knowing how to serve the Lord. But I have learned that as we are connected to Christ through faith, the Holy Spirit leads us to recognize the good that God is doing in our lives. Paul reminds us of this in Romans 8:28: "And we know that for those who love God all things work together for good, for those who are called according to His purpose." The last half of this verse opens our eyes to the idea that God, even when we don't know it or see it, is using us for His purpose, and our purpose is in Him. But what does this have to do with Psalm 116:15–16?

Looking at our lives across a chronological timeline, and not just at a single point in time, we can become more aware of God's power and blessing in our lives. I have learned that God does not falter in His gracious work for me. The same is true of what He graciously works for you. When I think about my position in my family as a younger sibling, excelling in high school and college further than I could have dreamed, overcoming the obstacles and hurdles that Satan put in my path—my own inclinations and selfish ambitions that, not too long ago, overran my mind, body, and spirit—I begin to realize and take hold of God's power, love, and grace in my life. God would not—He will never—let go of me, *ever*. And He will never let go of you. He will never leave me or forsake me, and He will never leave or forsake you. I know we hear that often, but really think about it. Just as God is all powerful, God's love in Christ is unconditional. In that light, thinking about our lives and pondering what, where, and how God is working for us and in us is, for me at least, incredibly humbling, and it leads me instantly to want to serve Him in thankfulness.

When I first read verse 15, "Precious in the sight of the LORD is the death of His saints," I wasn't sure exactly what to think. Why would my death be precious to God?

Now y'all are saying, "Mike thinks he's a saint!" But seriously, why is the death of God's servant precious? At first I thought that maybe their deaths are precious because when believers die, they are reunited with our Father in heaven. Before we try to understand more about that verse, let's first ask this question: what makes you or me precious to God in the first place?

As one reads more and more of God's Word, it becomes evident that we are precious to God in many ways. First, He is our Creator. In the Garden of Eden, God called all of His creation "good." That includes us humans. Second, God is our Redeemer. God not only created us, but through the sacrifice of His Son, Jesus Christ, God has forgiven all our sins. Third, God is our Sanctifier. He has promised each of us tremendous blessings. He gives us the opportunity for life to the fullest; He gives us the promises of salvation, the forgiveness of sins, and eternal life. He also begins to make us righteous, to conform us to Christ's image, through His Spirit. God made His promises of salvation in the Old Testament and confirmed them in Christ in the New Testament. Just how precious we are in God's sight can be seen in the death and resurrection of His Son.

At some time, everyone asks, "What is my purpose?" What is unique about that question is that every religion aims to answer it—every single one. I am not here to bash or try to completely dissemble another person's beliefs. I know what God the Father has revealed to me about Himself through His Word, and that His Spirit has cleansed my heart through faith in His Son. But I believe that that feeling we all have inside, that question "Why am I here?" is our initial calling from the God of all creation. By nature, every person knows that God exists, even if he or she denies it. Our lives have no real purpose without God in them. But with God in our lives—that is, being restored to a real relationship through faith in His Son—we can begin to understand how the deaths of God's children, including my death, are precious in His sight. He is our Creator, Redeemer, and Sanctifier. Everything that happens to us has a purpose; everything has meaning.

Let's look at verse 16: "O LORD, I am Your servant; I am Your servant, the son of Your maidservant. You have loosed my bonds." As I grow older, I realize more and more that my life is not about me. Where I have been, where I am now, and where I am going is all about God. I am a servant through obedience—obedience to God's direction and calling in my life, obedience to Christ, and directed by God's purpose for me which He makes clear in His Word. It is through this grace-enabled obedience and submission that I am made humble and able to graciously serve, which for me is not always an easy thing. I've come to realize the most freeing thing in my life isn't pursuing dreams on the field; it is not even the earthly success or other blessings from God's hand. I know that He can take away all of this in an instant. What is most important is that God has freed me from my chains through His Son, has called me by His Spirit, and enables me by His grace to fulfill my purpose on earth.

By responding to God's call through repentant faith in Jesus, we give praise to our heavenly Father. My death and your death are precious to our heavenly Father because everything about us is precious to Him. He has proven that by all He has done and continues to do for us. And when our work on earth is complete, when our purpose has been fulfilled, He will be pleased to welcome us to our heavenly home because His Son has set us free from all of our imperfections and sin.

....

By responding to God's call through repentant faith in Jesus, we give praise to our heavenly Father. My death and your death are precious to our heavenly Father because everything about us is precious to Him.

Prayer: Lord God, You have called me to faith in Your Son, Jesus Christ. Help me to use my time on earth for Your purposes, and when my time to depart this life comes, welcome me into Your heavenly kingdom. I ask this through Christ, my Lord. Amen.

....

DAILY STUDY QUESTIONS
Psalm 116:15–16

1. Though making lists can be hazardous, what would you include on a "Top Five Precious Possessions" list? What is it about the things on your list that make them precious?

2. Considering the context of the rest of the psalm, what is it about verse 15 that may seem a bit confusing?

3. What is your understanding of verse 15? How is the death of a saint *precious*?

4. How does one live as God's servant?

5. In the coming day, what changes can you make to better reflect God's attitude toward His godly ones (your fellow saints) and His call for you to serve them?

Psalm 116:17–19

I will offer to You the sacrifice of thanksgiving and call on the name of the LORD. I will pay my vows to the LORD in the presence of all His people, in the courts of the house of the LORD, in your midst, O Jerusalem. Praise the LORD!

A Sacrifice of Thanksgiving

Sometimes we discover that we can do amazing things. Society salutes our skills and performance. Newspapers highlight our names with bold lettering. We find fulfillment in the rewards we receive and the success we experience. There are even days when we stand higher than our own employer. We celebrate our victories with fireworks and confetti. Our individual successes drive our friendships and our relationships. The joy of this world comes from how great we are in front of other people. We love to hear our name blared from the stadium speakers as we run out of the tunnel and onto the field. We bow to crowds as they stand and cheer. We sit on the stage as the spotlight shines on us. I wonder, how does God feel as we bow to this world?

I guess it took me a long time in my career to understand that I didn't manufacture my own skills. Don't get me wrong; I have always tried to work as hard as possible. I believed that the harder I worked, the more I would be given. However, my experience is that that is not necessarily true. I do believe that "you get what you deserve," but I have also found that sometimes what we deserve may not be what we want, and we may get it when we don't want it. I also believe that you should never sacrifice what you want most for what you want now. Throughout my life, I have always wanted a quick return on my investment. I wanted the crowd to cheer for me or the spotlight to shine on me. Then I finally realized that what I want most is to spend eternity with my Lord and Savior, Jesus Christ. When I came to that realization, my life changed spiritually, and I also became more thankful. I thanked my peers for congratulating me and cheering for me. As a Christian, I realized that while I might be congratulated for some things, God is to be thanked for everything.

We offer Him our "sacrifice of thanksgiving," as the psalmist says in verse 17. God gives us everything we have and everything that we are able to do in our lives. It's His gift to us. Because of God's mercy, we can, as Paul says, give thanks "always and for everything to God the Father in the name of our Lord Jesus Christ" (Ephesians 5:20).

Because all of us are born with a sinful nature, we do not "naturally" give thanks. Truthfully, we do not deserve to live. However, God is gracious, giving us what we do not deserve. In fact, that is the definition of grace. In Christ, God gives us the grace to live instead of sentencing us to death. Because God's grace reprioritizes our lives, we can be thankful not only for big things, but also for all the simple things—even our very breath. God saves us from so much sorrow and pain. He sent His only Son to die on the cross so that we no longer have to live in vain. Our lives in Christ have meaning. That's why it's futile to complain about the tiniest problems we experience in life. In Christ, does it make sense to lose friends over arguments that mean nothing in the end? Should we allow our relationships to be ruined just because of a lack of communication? Isn't there great value in just sitting back and being thankful for what God has given us?

Paul wrote, "I thank my God in all my remembrance of you" (Philippians 1:3). Imagine if we instilled God-given thankfulness for what He has done for us in Christ into our marriages. Imagine if we turned the spotlight away from us to God. Imagine if the cheers were for Him and not for us: paying "[our] vows to the LORD in the presence of all His people," as the psalmist writes in verse 18. Do you think that such a life would be better? I can tell you from experience that it is. When the spotlight is focused on God, life is better. As I said, earlier in my career, I wanted to be in the spotlight. I craved the attention and the praise. At that time, my life never seemed to be stable; it had more ups and downs than a roller coaster. I would lose my temper so quickly that it wasn't even funny. Quick to complain and on the verge of hopelessness, my nights were sleepless and my relationships with other people were rocky. I can also look back and see how quickly I tried to finish playing with my kids, taking for granted what God has blessed me with. What I have learned is that God deserves the credit for everything that I do and for everything that is in my life. Life presents us with both good and bad. Our fallen world is not perfect, and neither are we. But with God's grace, we can nevertheless find the good in everything and give thanks to God for it.

Paul also says that we are to offer our bodies "as a living sacrifice, holy and acceptable to God, which is [our] spiritual worship" (Romans 12:1). God's grace in Christ enables us to offer our lives as thank-offerings. How we handle our lives and give praise and thanks to God in all that we do is our offering. The way we talk to people, the way we walk, the people we surround ourselves with, and even the words that come out of our mouths are all offerings to Christ. God's people see everything that we do, so perhaps it is time to start showing people what God is like. Perhaps it is time to show everyone through our actions that God is real, and that He is the Creator and Giver of all things.

What I am saying is this: bowing to God in repentant faith and thankful obedience is a lot better than being in the world's spotlight. Having true strength through faith in Jesus Christ is a lot better than being weak under Satan. Trumpets blaring at the gates of heaven will certainly sound better than the roar of earthly crowds. God gives us everything, and we can be thankful for it. Thanks be to God for His undeserved grace and the salvation He has given us through Jesus Christ. Praise the Lord!

....

What I am saying is this: bowing to God in repentant faith and thankful obedience is a lot better than being in the world's spotlight. . . . Trumpets blaring at the gates of heaven will certainly sound better than the roar of earthly crowds.

Prayer: Heavenly Father, forgive me for presuming that my skills and abilities are my creation. Thank You for giving me my unique gifts, and help me to use them to Your glory, so that others might be brought to saving faith in Christ. In His name I pray. Amen.

....

Friday

DAILY STUDY QUESTIONS
Psalm 116:17-19

1. What kind of praise and recognition is most meaningful to you? What makes you feel appreciated?

2. Is receiving praise for something you have done antithetical to giving God praise for what He has accomplished through you?

3. How do Christians offer sacrifices of thanksgiving to God?

4. Why is Jerusalem singled out by the psalmist (v. 19)? What "holy places" are special to you?

5. What responsibility do you as an individual have for the worship of the entire community of faith that is your congregation?

Week Three

....

Psalm 116

....

The 116th psalm is a psalm of thanks in which
the psalmist is joyful and gives thanks that God
has heard his prayer and has rescued him from
the distress of death and the anguish of hell.
Like several other psalms above, it speaks of the
deep spiritual affliction, of which few people
know. He laments in this psalm that things are
so bad, yet he confesses his faith and the truth
of God. He calls all human holiness, virtue, and
confidence only falsehood and emptiness. This
the world will not and cannot hear nor tolerate.
Thus it comes that the godly suffer, tremble,
and fear all kinds of misfortune. But despite
all, he is comforted by this, that God's Word is
true and will only motivate us the more: "They
give me to drink from the cup of their wrath.
All right, then I will take the cup of grace and
salvation and drink myself spiritually drunk and
(through preaching) pour out from this cup on
those who will drink with me and who draw
their grace from the Word." This is our cup, and
with this cup we will worship God and praise
His name. We will fulfill our vows, namely the
First Commandment, that we receive Him as the
one God and praise Him as the only God worthy
to preach and to be called upon. You find here
also that giving thanks, preaching, and confessing God's name before all people is the true
worship of God.

         —Martin Luther

Week Three, Psalm 116

GROUP BIBLE STUDY
(Questions and answers on pp. 200–203.)

1. What was your most recent encounter with death? How should Christians think about death?

2. The opening line of the psalm is exceedingly terse and vibrant in Hebrew, literally, "I love for Yahweh listens." How does this opening set the tone for the entire psalm? What does it teach us about the vitality of our relationship with God and about the way that we pray?

3. What makes a prayer a *good* prayer? How does the prayer of verse 4 measure up?

4. Looking around at the world and the sorts of things that you and others experience, what conclusions would you reach about God's character? How would you respond to someone who argued that he saw no evidence to support the claim of verse 5?

5. How would you describe a "simple" person? Why would God preserve such people (v. 6)? What would you think about trying to live your life more simply?

6. Overwhelmed by the stunning reality of God's grace, the psalmist asks the only polite—the only *possible*—question (v. 12). What do you think of his answer (vv. 13–14)? What relevance does his answer have for Christians today?

7. Twice (vv. 14 and 18), the psalmist asserts his commitment to pay his vows to the Lord and hopes that it may happen "in the presence of all His people." What does he have in mind? Why do you think this setting is so important to him? What should Christians learn from this today?

8. While the death of every creature is significant to the Creator (Matthew 10:29), what is it that makes the death of God's saints actually precious (v. 15)? Think about the attitude conveyed by the Church's practices; how might they better communicate the idea that the death of a believer is precious?

9. How is it true that verse 16 describes a move between two very different ways of being bound? What is binding you today?

10. When all is said and done, why is "Praise the LORD!" a very good way to end a prayer?

Week Four

Psalm 135

¹ Praise the LORD! Praise the name of the LORD,
give praise, O servants of the LORD,

² who stand in the house of the LORD,
in the courts of the house of our God!

³ Praise the LORD, for the LORD is good;
sing to His name, for it is pleasant!

⁴ For the LORD has chosen Jacob for Himself,
Israel as His own possession.

⁵ For I know that the LORD is great,
and that our Lord is above all gods.

⁶ Whatever the LORD pleases, He does,
in heaven and on earth,
in the seas and all deeps.

⁷ He it is who makes the clouds rise at the end of the earth,
who makes lightnings for the rain
and brings forth the wind from His storehouses.

⁸ He it was who struck down the firstborn of Egypt,
both of man and of beast;

⁹ who in your midst, O Egypt,
sent signs and wonders
against Pharaoh and all his servants;

¹⁰ who struck down many nations
and killed mighty kings,

¹¹ Sihon, king of the Amorites,
and Og, king of Bashan,
and all the kingdoms of Canaan,

¹² and gave their land as a heritage,
a heritage to His people Israel.

¹³ Your name, O Lord, endures forever,
Your renown, O Lord, throughout all ages.

¹⁴ For the Lord will vindicate His people
and have compassion on His servants.

¹⁵ The idols of the nations are silver and gold,
the work of human hands.

¹⁶ They have mouths, but do not speak;
they have eyes, but do not see;

¹⁷ they have ears, but do not hear,
nor is there any breath in their mouths.

¹⁸ Those who make them become like them,
so do all who trust in them!

¹⁹ O house of Israel, bless the Lord!
O house of Aaron, bless the Lord!

²⁰ O house of Levi, bless the Lord!
You who fear the Lord, bless the Lord!

²¹ Blessed be the Lord from Zion,
He who dwells in Jerusalem!
Praise the Lord!

Fred Gaede

Psalm 135:1–4

> Praise the LORD! Praise the name of the LORD, give praise, O servants of the LORD, who stand in the house of the LORD, in the courts of the house of our God! Praise the LORD, for the LORD is good; sing to His name, for it is pleasant! For the LORD has chosen Jacob for Himself, Israel as His own possession.

Praise the Lord

Praise the Lord! Praise Him, praise Him, praise Him! It sure seems that the writer of Psalm 135 has a lot to be happy about. What could bring out this much praise? The first three verses have everyone praising the Lord not just because He is good, which He is, but because He has chosen Jacob and Israel. Well, my name isn't Jacob, and I was born a few miles outside Chicago, Illinois.

I remember too many times when "getting chosen" didn't seem like such a good thing, so I guess I'm off the hook.

I remember getting "chosen" to go into the high school football game after the first-string lineman got injured by the opposing team. Yes, I had wanted to go into the game, I had wanted to show the coach what I could do, but not against *that* team. Those guys were massive.

Years later, I was "chosen" to be on the youth board at our church. "It's an honor to be chosen," my wife told me. Next thing I knew I was in a bus full of rowdy junior high students on a two-hour trip to Wisconsin. I was "honored" to spend three nights chasing boys out of girls' dorm rooms and becoming hoarse from shouting "Lights out was at eleven!" until five thirty in the morning.

As an adult, I was "chosen" to head an important project. I knew that my company's reputation *and* my job were on the line. Great. Thanks for choosing me.

What it really comes down to, I guess, is what you are being chosen for and who is doing the choosing.

We know from Psalm 135 that the Lord has chosen Jacob, and that He has chosen Israel. The task Jacob was chosen for seems pretty huge when compared with some of the tasks that have been set before us. Genesis 28 tells us that Abraham's covenant was perpetuated through Jacob—that it would be Jacob's descendants who would spread throughout the earth, and that all people would be blessed through him and his offspring.

When the Old Testament covenant was fulfilled in Christ Jesus and He instituted the new covenant, we got swept up in Jacob's task. We've been chosen too. Look at John 15:16: "You did not choose Me, but I chose you and appointed that you should go and bear fruit and that your fruit should abide." We also read in Ephesians 1:4 that "He chose us in Him before the foundation of the world, that we should be holy and blameless before Him."

Yes, we've been chosen. Not by our boss or our old football coach. Not for some task or drudgery, but for eternal life, so that even now we are holy and blameless before God through faith in His Son, and we bear fruit to His glory.

I'll be honest with you. At times, this seems like too big a task for a man like me. Just like all those years ago when I had to go into that football game, I'd rather pass this time, please. Back then, I really had no choice. The coach had called me to go in, and go in I did. I can still remember taking my stance on the field and looking into the faces of the other players. They were huge. Honestly. I tried my best to look tough. I tried to growl and look mean, but I think I might have actually whimpered. The count was shouted, and at the snap of the ball I was off, launching myself into a solid wall of muscle. This wall tossed me aside and I was in our backfield in a matter of seconds. Luckily, we had gotten our pass off. Then I had to do it again. I might have lasted a quarter before the coach wisely pulled me out and went to the third string to finish the game.

Now, if I was unable to serve in something as insignificant as a high school football game, how can I possibly serve the Lord God Almighty and do what He asks of us? Seriously, God, can't You do better than me? Isn't there someone more qualified? Maybe You should skip me and move on to the third string.

But Scripture is very clear, isn't it? "He chose us in [Christ] before the foundation of the world." Through my Baptism, this includes me. What's even more amazing is the fact that He has sent us His Counselor, the Holy Spirit (John 14:16–17, 26), who is better than any coach, trainer, or manager could ever hope to be. With the faith that the Holy Spirit gives us and strengthens in us, we can say, like Paul in Philippians 4:13, "I can do all things through Him who strengthens me." And just as the Lord did when Moses questioned Him for choosing Moses to deliver Israel out of Egypt, the Lord promises to be with us.

When bearing the name of Christ seems like a burden—when we doubt and say to ourselves, why me, Lord? Why did You have to choose me and put me into these circumstances?—we would do well to remember just who it is who has chosen us. It is the Lord of Jacob. It is the same Lord who gave Moses the power to lead the Israelites out of Egypt. It is the same Lord who gave out the Holy Spirit at Pentecost. It is this same Lord who has chosen us and will stand by us and give us strength.

So when we are placed in situations where we are asked to "bear fruit" or be a living example of Christ to our fellowman, we can act with confidence and surety, knowing that He is with us. Through the Word and Sacraments, He is actually part of us. We can stand with the whole Church as the very Body of Christ. That old immovable wall from the football game is no longer a threat. We can run onto the field and out into the world with confidence. Now I know full well who has chosen me: the most holy triune God; and I know what I have been chosen for: eternal life; so even now, I bear fruit and am holy before Him. I know that His choice of me in Christ assures me of eternal life. I have nothing to be afraid of. All these things are truly worth the praises in the first three verses of Psalm 135: "Praise the LORD! Praise the name of the LORD, give praise."

....

So when we are placed in situations where we are asked to "bear fruit" or be a living example of Christ to our fellowman, we can act with confidence and surety, knowing that He is with us.

Prayer: Heavenly Father, I thank and praise You that You have chosen me to eternal life. Forgive me for my fears and shortcomings. Strengthen me with Your Holy Spirit so that I daily remember my Baptism and rest in the assurance that You are always with me. In Jesus' name. Amen.

....

DAILY STUDY QUESTIONS
Psalm 135:1–4

1. What's the most difficult job you've had to do that seemed to choose *you*, perhaps in spite of your desires or instincts?

2. Why was Jacob—and with him, the whole people of Israel—chosen by God?

3. What two reasons does the psalmist offer as motivation for the praise that should be given to God? How are they different?

4. What do you think: are the first and final words of the psalm a command, an acclamation, a spontaneous prayer, or simply an expression of delight?

5. When did God choose you? What does that choice have to do with your worship life today?

Week Four Tuesday

Psalm 135:5–7

> For I know that the LORD is great, and that our Lord is above all gods. Whatever the LORD pleases, He does, in heaven and on earth, in the seas and all deeps. He it is who makes the clouds rise at the end of the earth, who makes lightnings for the rain and brings forth the wind from His storehouses.

Count on Him

"I know. I know. I know." So often have I heard those words from my sons—usually after they had been caught doing something they shouldn't have been doing. "I know we're not supposed to play ball indoors." "I know I should have started my homework last week." "I know I wasn't supposed to have everyone over while you and Mom were away." The list goes on and on. What usually comes after "I know"? The famous word *but*. "I know that I shouldn't have done that, *but* . . . ." ". . . *but* it wasn't my fault. The other guys said I could do it."

My standard fatherly response was "If you knew it was wrong, why did you still do it?" Sound familiar? I guess it's just part of growing up. It's also part of raising children. When I first read Psalm 135:5–7, I was struck by the words "For I know that the LORD is great." They hit me a little close to the heart.

When I stop to think about it, I'm a lot like my two boys. I know that the Lord is great—*but*. But I put other "gods" before our one triune God.

In reading these verses, we see just how great our God truly is. He is above all other gods; He does what He pleases in heaven and on earth. He controls every aspect of our natural world. Through the faith given to me by the Holy Spirit, I *know* this!

So the question is, just as it was with my boys, if I know this, why don't I act accordingly? Like the psalmist, I know how great this God is. I know of His Old and New Testament power and love. I know how that great love was brought to us through His most precious Son, Jesus Christ. I know how Jesus took all my sins to the cross so that I may be washed clean in the blood of His forgiveness. I know this, and what's more, I *believe* it.

But . . .

But I daily drop the ball and do stupid things. I daily push Him into the background and push myself forward, taking care of things in my own way. What these daily failings really mean is that I do not put the one true God above all my other gods.

The concept of "other gods" was made very clear to me a few months back. During this recent economic downturn, the company I was working for had a number of clients whose businesses suffered severe losses. Work we had counted on suddenly stopped coming. Work we had been expecting in the future never came in. This meant a drastic loss of billings for us. It's obvious to see what comes next. Our company, of which I was part owner, had to react quickly or go out of business. I was faced with the reality of being out of a job. In order to survive, we had to make sacrifices. Unfortunately, we had to lay off employees. We had to cut our own salaries drastically. We had to look closely at every expense, no matter how small.

When my wife and I looked at our own lifestyle, we realized we had to do the same thing. Every expense was examined. It was at this time that all my "other gods" came out of hiding. Many things we took for granted or thought of as part of our lifestyle were scrutinized. I looked at all my stuff—stuff that did nothing but take my eyes away from what truly mattered. Why did I need two sets of golf clubs? I could hardly break 100 with one set, let alone two. And televisions! They were in the den, bedroom, basement, and kids' room. Don't even *ask* me about guitars. I had enjoyed the fruits of my income, and I had spent like it would never end. My confidence was in me and in *my* ability to provide. I was forgetting that it is the triune God who is in control.

Now, I know that there's nothing awful here, nothing that would get the neighbors talking. But while that may be true, I came to realize that my "other gods" were really just one: myself. I was putting myself and the things I wanted, or thought I needed, above my Lord. I was more concerned about pleasing myself than Him. I had easily pushed Him off to one side while I took control.

"I know, I know, *but . . .*"

Now it is my heavenly Father's turn to say, "If you knew it was wrong, why did you still do it?"

If I held my "self-godliness" up against His supreme Godliness, there would be no contest. This could be a terrifying prospect. Certainly that is so when we read in these verses just how powerful our God is, and that "whatever the Lord pleases, He does." How thankful I am that we have the one true God and that He loves us so much, more than we can even imagine. He loves us so much that He sent us His only Son to atone for all our sins. Even when we act like we know more than He does, He continues to love us—and He wants us to be with Him! It pleases Him to have us spend eternity with Him, sharing in His marriage feast of the Lamb!

I now daily pray that I never forget just who our God is. I thank and praise Him that He is in control of every aspect of my life, and I ask for forgiveness whenever I find myself thinking that I know of a better way than His. Even when careers and personal situations seem out of control, I know He can be counted on.

How thankful I am that we have the one true God and that He loves us so much, more than we can even imagine. He loves us so much that He sent us His only Son to atone for all our sins.

Prayer: Dear Lord, thank You for loving a selfish sinner like me. Forgive me for trusting in myself instead of You and for rebelling against Your wisdom, despite Your power and great might. You alone, O Lord, are great and are above all gods, O God of love. In Jesus' name I pray. Amen.

Tuesday

DAILY STUDY QUESTIONS
Psalm 135:5–7

1. What are some of the gods that have been competing for the top spot in your life lately?

2. If you knew what was right and good to do, why did you do the opposite? What's the only honest response to this question? How rational is sin?

3. How do you know that Yahweh is great and above all other gods?

4. As the psalmist describes Yahweh's creative work, what do you learn about God's relationship with the created realm? How involved is God in the happenings of this world?

5. What evidence of God's activity in your immediate world have you witnessed lately (or what can you see when you learn to look for it) that gives you reason to praise God today?

Psalm 135:8-12

> He it was who struck down the firstborn of Egypt, both of
> man and of beast; who in your midst, O Egypt, sent signs and
> wonders against Pharaoh and all his servants; who struck down
> many nations and killed mighty kings, Sihon, king of the Amor-
> ites, and Og, king of Bashan, and all the kingdoms of Canaan,
> and gave their land as a heritage, a heritage to His people
> Israel.

Our Almighty Father

It may sound kind of trite, but I can honestly say that my earthly hero and role model is my dad. I consider myself blessed to have been raised by him and to have had him in my life for as long as I have lived. Now that he is in his late seventies and I'm in my fifties, our relationship has changed, but he is still the one I look to for advice and inspiration. When I look back over the years, I tend to remember many enjoyable times. I remember riding in his milk truck, sleeping out in the old shed in our backyard, and a classic game or two of catch. It's only when I get together with my sisters and we begin to reminisce that I remember my dad ever being angry. I tend not to think of my dad as being angry or stern. I guess I just don't like to.

These next few verses of Psalm 135 reminded me of this side of my earthly father. There certainly were times when my father exercised his authority. Back then, I guess, we thought he was angry or mean when he did so. These verses also remind all of us of the powerful, mighty side of our heavenly Father. We enjoy thinking of our Lord as loving and gentle. Certainly this is the popular side of Jesus in today's society. But let's look at verse 8: "He it was who struck down the firstborn of Egypt, both of man and of beast"; and then verses 9 and 10: ". . . who in your midst, O Egypt, sent signs and wonders against Pharaoh and all his servants; who struck down many nations and killed mighty kings." This certainly sounds like a stern and angry God. As with my father, I usually don't like to think of this side of our Savior.

It's only when I think back a little harder, or study the Bible a little bit more diligently, that I am able to see past my own selfish thoughts. The times when my earthly father was angry or stern were times when I crossed him or didn't do what he told me to do. How true this is with our heavenly Father as well. Exodus 7–14 tells us of the many times the Lord tried to convince Pharaoh to free the children of Israel, but Pharaoh chose not to listen. Now, I don't know about your relationship with your dad, but if I had chosen not to listen to mine when he told me at least six times to do something, I would have been in big trouble. I was never struck or abused, but I was punished. And in each instance that I can recall, I simply got what I deserved.

I have sometimes gotten angry with my sons when they do things that could hurt them physically, emotionally, or spiritually. I get even angrier at the temptations and evils in this world that are constantly working to lead them astray. Because I love my children so much, I would do everything in my power to protect and defend them. But of course, my power is quite limited, and my anger is most often misdirected.

How thankful I am that our heavenly Father is who He is. He is the God above all gods. He loves us, His children, more deeply than I could even imagine loving my two boys. And He hates our enemies—sin, the devil, and the flesh—with equal passion. We are so blessed to be His children. In verse 12, after His angry, powerful actions have been related, we see His purpose for doing them. He did them for His children, Israel. He conquered their enemies so that they could have their heritage.

We can see this ourselves in the most glorious expression of God's love, His Son, Jesus Christ. Through His all-encompassing death and resurrection, the enemies of sin and death have been conquered. Through Holy Baptism, we have been brought into the family of God, and our heritage, our inheritance, is eternal life.

Yes, it's nice to think back to the fun days with my dad, when he was my friend and catch partner, but that would be shortchanging all that he did for me. He and my Mom struggled and sacrificed for the benefit of our family. They protected us, taught us, and disciplined us. They raised us up to be Christian fathers and mothers to our own children. And all of this they did because they loved us. There were fun times, of course, but there were also times of stern authority. Even today, when we are together, my father deserves and receives my admiration, respect, and obedience.

Likewise, to only think of our God as a kind, gentle, meek, mild buddy would be a great disservice to Him. Yes, Jesus loves me, but He loves so much that He conquers our foes, disciplines us, teaches us, and leads us in ways we can never imagine. Above all, He made the ultimate sacrifice for us. He carried our sins to the cross and conquered them so that we might live.

Truly, our almighty heavenly Father, with His Son, Jesus Christ, and the Holy Spirit are worthy of the utmost praise!

....

Likewise, to only think of our God as a kind and gentle, meek and mild buddy would be a great disservice to Him. Yes, Jesus loves me, but He loves so much that He conquers our foes, disciplines us, teaches us, and leads us in ways we can never imagine.

Prayer: Dear God, thank You for bringing me into the Your family. Please protect me and all Your children from the temptations and evils of the world. Strengthen me through Your Spirit, and keep me always walking in the ways of Your Son, Jesus Christ. In His name I pray. Amen.

....

DAILY STUDY QUESTIONS
Psalm 135:8–12

1. What are the strongest memories you have of your father? Is having "selective memories" dishonest and self-deceptive, or is it a way of honoring those we love?

2. How might the wrath of God be both terrifying and reassuring?

3. The psalmist happily recounts the fact that God smote Pharaoh and a few other kings who were foolish enough to threaten His plan for Israel. How has this kind of divine activity changed with the coming of Christ?

4. Verses 6 and 7 proclaim the power of God within creation in general. What is the effect of the specific, historical recounting of God's power that follows in verses 8–11?

5. What is the heritage that you have been given as a child and heir of God (v. 12)?

Psalm 135:13-18

Your name, O LORD, endures forever, Your renown, O LORD, throughout all ages. For the LORD will vindicate His people and have compassion on His servants. The idols of the nations are silver and gold, the work of human hands. They have mouths, but do not speak; they have eyes, but do not see; they have ears, but do not hear, nor is there any breath in their mouths. Those who make them become like them, so do all who trust in them!

God's Name
Endures Forever

I have always been interested in cemeteries. Not in a morbid way, by any means, but simply because of the history and stories they have to tell. In my hometown there are two cemeteries in particular that I find fascinating. I can walk three or four blocks there and look at the plot and headstone of my great-great-grandfather. If I go another half mile or so, I can see the plot of my grandfather. Both of these men share my own first and last names. There is a rose-colored marble headstone over my great-great-grandfather's plot that has a brief line in German about our family coming over from the Fatherland. The stone was placed there close to a century ago, but it looks as if it were just recently carved.

Every October our town has what they call a "Talking Tombstones" evening at this cemetery. Local historians select four or five headstones to research, and they study the history of those persons or families. On "Talking Tombstones" night, they dress in period costume and act out these people's stories—who they were, where they came from, and what they did in our small town. It's an enjoyable evening that brings history to life and makes one appreciate the struggles and labors of those who have gone before us.

But these historians can only research the names they can read off of the stones. They can only dig into history that is on file and recorded somewhere. If one walks a few paces from my family's headstone, you can't help but run into scores of other, smaller stones that go back even further into the past. Unfortunately, many of the names have eroded off these headstones. The dates are fading as well. In some areas, they are nothing more than white marble slabs with no discernible information on them. I have to ask myself, who is telling *their* story? I'm sure these people would have been interesting to know. Hidden beneath these blank slabs must be some unique and remarkable tales. Somebody knew them and loved them enough to place a carved stone memorial over their graves.

We all want to be remembered after we've passed on. It would be nice to know that we won't be forgotten after our children or grandchildren have passed away. I must admit that I've given some thought to what I'd like to have carved on my tombstone. There are two or three messages that I've been kicking around, but I think I'm settling on "Having a wonderful time, wish you were here."

But honestly, what does it matter? As Christian men, our purpose is not to memorialize ourselves, but to glorify our Lord and Savior, Jesus Christ. As I stand in these cemeteries, fascinating as they are, I can't help but think of how I'm surrounded by lifeless people memorialized by lifeless stones. No matter how big the headstone or mausoleum, if it's not "Talking Tombstone" night, there are only death and fading memories here.

In verse 13, the psalmist tells us that our Lord's memorial will stand for all eternity. His name won't fade with time or memory. Here we see that the name of the Lord will endure forever and that His memorial will stand for all generations—not just one or two, but *all* generations. This glorious God who does what He pleases in all the earth, who controls the wind and rain, who smites great nations and does all this because He loves His children so much—this majestic God will stand forever.

While the memorials and idols of men are lifeless and silent, His is a living and active memorial. It's a memorial that speaks the living Word, the Word that changes lives and saves souls. It's an active memorial that showers us in the baptismal waters and feeds us His very body and blood. It's a memorial that wraps us up in His love and teaches and prepares us to go out and bring others into this marvelous fellowship. It's a memorial that actively includes us in all of His power and glory. It turns us into His very own "Talking Tombstones," telling and showing His story of love and forgiveness to those who need this life-giving Word.

Yes, our personal names, photos, videos, and stories will fade. But the one thing we have that will never fade is the title *Christian*. By being part of the living Body of Christ, His Church, we are, in fact, eternal. Even now, when times seem tough and we struggle to make our way in this earthly kingdom, the Spirit reminds us that we are everlasting. Our inheritance is in His heavenly kingdom. Christ knows us by name, and He certainly won't forget us!

As I'm writing this devotion, there's an old western movie playing on television. One of the many clichés of these films is the dramatic death scene in which one of the characters dies in the hero's arms. Then he's usually buried in a shallow grave with a simple cross of sticks placed over his head. Maybe this is the greatest earthly memorial one can leave. No name, no clever sayings, no dates—simply the cross. To die in Christ in the hope of the resurrection, leaving behind the story of His all-atoning sacrifice for the world's sins, is a life well lived.

....

Yes, our personal names, photos, videos, and stories will fade. But the one thing we have that will never fade is the title of *Christian*. By being part of the living Body of Christ, His Church, we are, in fact, eternal.

Prayer: Lord Jesus Christ, thank You for the Christian men in my life who have shown me how to live. Take away the idols in my life, and guide my heart and mind so what I say and do may please You. I ask this in Your name. Amen.

....

DAILY STUDY QUESTIONS
Psalm 135:13–18

1. What tombstones have special significance for you? What story would you want your own tombstone to tell?

2. How are tombstones and idols alike?

3. In your experience, what idols seem to be getting the most attention from people today?

4. How do the two "halves" of verse 14 fit together? Are they saying the same thing, contradicting each other, or stating two unrelated thoughts?

5. What does verse 18 teach you about the immediate consequences of trusting idols?

Psalm 135:19–21

> O house of Israel, bless the LORD! O house of Aaron, bless the LORD! O house of Levi, bless the LORD! You who fear the LORD, bless the LORD! Blessed be the LORD from Zion, He who dwells in Jerusalem! Praise the LORD!

Worthy of Praise

I was riding my bike today and took a side trip past the Little League fields in the park near our home. When my boys were younger, we spent every weekend at this park watching their Little League teams. I think we spent twelve summers in a row watching the two of them play baseball. It was great fun, and we met some wonderful people. There were only a few championship years that I can recall. What I do remember well is all the cheering and yelling. I was always amazed at just how enthusiastic a parent could be when it came to cheering the team. I remember many of the standard cheers: "Let's get some runs!" "Good job, infield! Keep it up!" "Relax, kiddo, just put the bat on the ball!"

I don't know if any of it really helped. If you talk to my boys, they'll tell you that they didn't pay much attention to any of the shouts coming from the parents' bleachers. When the team knew that they were not performing well, no amount of cheering helped. And when they were winning, they were doing their own yelling and shouting. Win or lose, we parents were proud and happy for our team. We were always full of praise for how they played and conducted themselves.

As we come to the end of Psalm 135 and the end of our week of study, we see the psalmist calling for praises to the God of Israel. Much like the opening verses of the psalm, we read that everyone is to join in praising our God. Our triune God, the God of creation, the God of Israel, has seen fit to call us His children and allows us to share in His glory through His blessed Son, Jesus Christ. Yes, He truly is worthy to be praised.

So the question is, how do we go about praising Him? The easy answer is to praise Him with our songs and voices during our weekly worship. Sometimes we might sing along to hymns of praise on our MP3 players, CD players, or car radios during the week. These are truly great ways to praise our Lord, but I think we are talking about something deeper here, a praise that goes beyond our usual understanding. In reading these verses, we see that all those assembled in the temple are called upon to "Bless the Lord!" The "house of Israel" (the entire congregation), the "house[s] of Aaron . . . [and] Levi" (the priests and ministers), and all "who fear the Lord" (even us today) are called upon to praise Him.

Assembled with this group of believers, how can we best praise our Lord? Simple "cheering" just doesn't seem to cut it. Just shouting "Good job, God! Keep up the good work!" seems too much like a Little League cheer. Back in those baseball days, we would cheer and raise our voices whether we believed we could win or not. It was just part of the game. But God certainly doesn't want our empty praise. He doesn't want us to simply sing songs just because they're part of service.

Thinking back over the years, I try to recall the highest form of praise I have ever received—and I'll be honest, there's not too much to be proud of. Actually, the highest praise I have ever received was not a direct compliment for me. It was when someone told me how impressed he or she was with my children's behavior.

There was the summer-camp counselor who said he wouldn't have been able to complete the weeklong canoe trip if it hadn't been for the help of my son John. It had been a rainy week, and John helped some of the canoeists keep their spirits up and not be afraid of the storms. Then there was the co-worker of mine who hired my son Matt to do some work and then made a point of telling me how hard a worker he was, outperforming his two nephews who had been hired for the same task. He was most impressed with Matt's lack of complaining.

To me, these examples constituted high praise, not because of the words spoken but because of the actions of my sons. I saw that they had listened to my wife's and my teachings and then had put them into practice.

Isn't this the highest praise for our heavenly Father as well? Not just our words, but putting His Word into action? What our Lord desires most is to bring us all back to paradise, and He has welcomed us into His plan. Through the power of the Holy Spirit, He sends us out into the world to share the Gospel and deliver acts of kindness to those in need. We praise Him most when we live in His Word, follow His path, and rejoice in His gifts.

So, while it truly is wonderful to sing in praise of His mighty works, it is also important to get out and *do* His work. I pray that God the Holy Spirit lifts and guides you so that the glorious story of salvation through Jesus Christ may be shared through each and every one of you.

....

What our Lord desires most is to bring us all back to paradise, and He has welcomed us into His plan. Through the power of the Holy Spirit, He sends us out into the world to share the Gospel and deliver acts of kindness to those in need.

Prayer: Dear Jesus, through Your death and resurrection, You set me free from sin. Grant me wisdom and courage to share Your Gospel with those I meet so that with them, I may sing Your praise forever in Your Father's kingdom. In Your name I pray. Amen.

....

DAILY STUDY QUESTIONS
Psalm 135:19–21

1. What's the highest praise you can recall personally receiving?

2. How is it possible for praise to be something less than wonderful and positive?

3. What is the difference between praising God and blessing God?

4. The psalmist is fond of the literary device of repetition. How does the repetition in verses 19 and 20 strengthen and intensify the message of these verses?

5. Why do you think the psalmist makes a point of mentioning Zion and Jerusalem? What holy places prompt you to praise merely by thinking of them?

Week Four

....

....

Psalm 135

....

The 135th psalm is a psalm of thanks. It calls
the priests to give thanks, preach, and praise
God for the wonders that He showed to the
people in Egypt and Canaan, so that they never
forget God and seek idols or other gods. This
happens when one does not occupy oneself
with—and diligently hold to—preaching and the
praise of God, as it says in the next psalm. But
where His Word is silenced and He does not
judge or teach, there truly shall be great anger
and no grace. Therefore think, you servants in
the house of the Lord, and preach diligently of
God and His works.

—Martin Luther

GROUP BIBLE STUDY
(Questions and answers on pp. 209–212.)

1. Tell the group about a situation when you were genuinely afraid or in serious danger. How might it be possible for those kinds of memories to become a part of the praises you offer to God?

2. The psalmist exhorts praise from the "servants of the LORD" who stand in the house and courts of God (vv. 1–2). Who might these people be? Why would *they* need to be encouraged to offer praise?

3. If we and the psalmist are strict monotheists (and we *are*), then what is meant in verse 5 by declaring Yahweh "above all gods"?

4. Verse 6 is quite striking in the simple and definitive declaration it makes: God does what He wants. How does this truth resonate with you? Does it encourage you? humble you? terrify you? What kind of problems does this bold truth raise?

5. Verses 6–14 are quite deliberate in their progression. What is the overall course of the "argument" in these verses? How does this parallel our own confessions of faith? What does this have to do with our praise of God?

6. Why was the giving of the land so significant to the people of Israel (v. 12)? What relevance does this have for Christians who praise God with this psalm?

7. If idols are merely and obviously the products of men, and men clearly know this, why do men continue to give them their attention and worship?

8. How does the repetitive structure of verses 16–17 work to strengthen the psalmist's point? What point does he make in verse 18? Why is this true, and what warning does it have for people today?

9. What is being conveyed by the three separate exhortations to the "houses" of Israel, Aaron, and Levi in verses 19–20? What might this threefold exhortation say to those today who wrestle with the relationship between the laity and the clergy?

10. What is the best way to praise (or bless) God? Is it possible to praise Him if the worship is habitual or rote? Do actions praise God better than songs?

Week Five

Psalm 145

[1] I will extol You, my God and King,
and bless Your name forever and ever.

[2] Every day I will bless You
and praise Your name forever and ever.

[3] Great is the LORD, and greatly to be praised,
and His greatness is unsearchable.

[4] One generation shall commend Your works to another,
and shall declare Your mighty acts.

[5] On the glorious splendor of Your majesty,
and on Your wondrous works, I will meditate.

[6] They shall speak of the might of Your awesome deeds,
and I will declare Your greatness.

[7] They shall pour forth the fame of Your abundant goodness
and shall sing aloud of Your righteousness.

[8] The LORD is gracious and merciful,
slow to anger and abounding in steadfast love.

[9] The LORD is good to all,
and His mercy is over all that He has made.

[10] All Your works shall give thanks to You, O LORD,
and all Your saints shall bless You!

[11] They shall speak of the glory of Your kingdom
and tell of Your power,

[12] to make known to the children of man Your mighty deeds,
and the glorious splendor of Your kingdom.

¹³ Your kingdom is an everlasting kingdom,
and Your dominion endures throughout all generations.

[The Lᴏʀᴅ is faithful in all His words
and kind in all His works.]

¹⁴ The Lᴏʀᴅ upholds all who are falling
and raises up all who are bowed down.

¹⁵ The eyes of all look to You,
and You give them their food in due season.

¹⁶ You open Your hand;
You satisfy the desire of every living thing.

¹⁷ The Lᴏʀᴅ is righteous in all His ways
and kind in all His works.

¹⁸ The Lᴏʀᴅ is near to all who call on Him,
to all who call on Him in truth.

¹⁹ He fulfills the desire of those who fear Him;
He also hears their cry and saves them.

²⁰ The Lᴏʀᴅ preserves all who love Him,
but all the wicked He will destroy.

²¹ My mouth will speak the praise of the Lᴏʀᴅ,
and let all flesh bless His holy name forever and ever.

Josh Salzberg

Psalm 145:1–3

> I will extol You, my God: and King, and bless Your name for-
> ever and ever. Every day I will bless You and praise Your name
> forever and ever. Great is the LORD, and greatly to be praised,
> and His greatness is unsearchable.

The Red Magnet

It was just a toy.

But my dad never received gifts from his parents, so when they asked what he'd like for his eighth birthday, a wise choice was of utmost importance. The question had been plaguing him for some time. One toy. What's it going to be?

You'd think the decision would have been relatively easy. This was 1967, after all. Atari wouldn't release their first video-game console for another ten years. Even if the Pong playing system had been available, his parents wouldn't have been willing or able to shell out $200 for a birthday gift.

That time period's equivalent of today's top-selling computer game was the Etch A Sketch. It had been released and made popular just a few years earlier, and almost every kid my father knew had one of the shiny red drawing machines. And if someone at school didn't have one, it would likely be on their wish list in time for Christmas.

An Etch A Sketch would be nice, of course—but that's not what caught my father's eye. No, his sights were set on something more versatile, more powerful.

His sights were set on a magnet.

It's possible my father was subconsciously mindful of his family's financial situation. Or perhaps he was showing an early interest in science and the laws of physics. Or maybe he was just easily entertained. I don't know what possessed him to want a magnet, but he did—badly.

And so the day came. There was no buildup, no fanfare. There wasn't even wrapping paper, but that didn't detract from my dad's excitement when he was handed his gift: a magnet. But this wasn't just *any* magnet. This magnet was in the form of a blond, blue-eyed bodybuilder, muscles nearly bursting through his red singlet. Surely this magnet was one of a kind.

Could it stick to the refrigerator? the sink? the door?

His scientific study went on for hours before it happened. Nearly every surface in the apartment—magnetic and otherwise—had been tested when suddenly, mysteriously, the magnet lost its transfixing properties.

That's not to say the muscle man stopped working. His effect on paper clips was as strong as ever. No, it was the magnet's effect on my dad that had worn off. The present he'd longed for and hoped for had lost all appeal within a matter of hours.

I'm sure it was no easy task, after turning the burly weight lifter over in his hands, after thinking through his options, to face his father and ask if he could trade in the red magnet for an Etch A Sketch.

Whatever smile might have been on my grandfather's face disappeared. My dad didn't know what would come next. Would he be punished for making such a bold request?

My father's father was a salesman, more akin to Willy Loman than the guy who sells orange-scented cleaning products on TV. He worked long hours, came home, and collapsed into an open-eyed coma in his reclining chair at the end of every day. This routine left little room for father-son interaction. In fact, most of my dad's evenings were spent throwing a baseball against the side of the apartment—alone—hoping the persistent thuds would beckon his father outside.

But although the words were never spoken, he knew his father loved him. After all, that's what parents do. They love their children. But the absence of those words left room for speculation. It would be nice to know—to see his love in some tangible way.

David's opening lines of Psalm 145 bring similar thoughts to mind. I'm happy for David, I really am. I'm thrilled he has a reason to praise God. I'm ecstatic he has some evidence of God's love in his life.

But the truth is, it often takes all my energy to merely mutter the exultation and glory of church songs without raising a fist to the heavens and shouting:

"Where are You?!"

"If You love me, show it!"

"If You want my praise, You're going to have to earn it!"

This sounds harsh, but is it such a crazy conversation to have? The Bible is filled with people who have experiences with God. I'm talking about real-life, talking-to-bushes, dropping-bread-from-the-sky kinds of experiences. How do I know that God is out there, let alone a God who actively loves me?

It would be nice to know—to see His love in some tangible way.

As unsure of God's love as I may be, my dad was just as sure that whatever love his father held for him disappeared with the return of the red magnet. He knew he had disappointed his father. He had broken their trust. He shouldn't have asked for the Etch A Sketch.

It was this guilt and regret that filled my dad's eight-year-old mind as he came home from school days later. Much to his surprise, and with no explanation, there on the kitchen table rested a shiny red drawing machine: an Etch A Sketch.

His dad gave him a new gift—even though he didn't deserve it, even though their family might or might not have had the money.

Even though he'd already gotten what he wanted.

My grandpa has been dead for years, but to this day, my father recalls that birthday. Even though fifty years have passed, it is *that* birthday, *that* Etch A Sketch®, which my dad looks to as vivid, unshakable evidence of his father's love.

I know I'm no different from that eight-year-old. I want what I want out of life. And what I want out of life is on my own terms, and it's constantly changing. But years ago, much to humanity's surprise, and with no explanation, there, in an animal's feeding trough, rested a tiny baby boy: God made flesh.

"In this the love of God was made manifest among us, that God sent His only Son into the world, so that we might live through Him" (1 John 4:9).

There's no question Jesus' death was a testament to the depth of His love. His resurrection secured our place in God's heart. And yet, it's funny how something as seemingly simple as a peasant birth, His step down from the throne of heaven, can move us.

It's often difficult to utter praise, and I genuinely believe God understands and empathizes with our doubt, but two millennia later, it is that birth, when God stepped into humanity, which we can look to as vivid, unshakable evidence of our heavenly Father's love.

If you think this isn't sign enough, if you think this isn't undeniable proof of

God's love for humanity, if you think it was just a birth . . .

   Then tell my dad it was just a toy.

··

The Bible is filled with people who have experiences with God. I'm talking about real-life, talking-to-bushes, dropping-bread-from-the-sky kinds of experiences. How do I know that God is out there, let alone a God who actively loves me?

Prayer: Heavenly Father, You are worthy of praise because You have sent Your Son, my Savior, Jesus Christ. Through Your Word, remind me every day of Your mercy and Your continual care for me that will last forever and ever. I ask this in Jesus' name. Amen.

··

Monday

DAILY STUDY QUESTIONS
Psalm 145:1-3

1. When have you received a gift that far surpassed what you expected or deserved?

2. What evidence do you have of God's unmerited grace and favor to you?

3. David twice declares that he will bless and praise the Lord "forever and ever." What assurance of faith might we read into this assertion?

4. How is this devotion itself a fulfillment of David's declaration/exhortation in verse 4?

5. What works of God do *you* need to talk to the next generation about today?

Psalm 145:4–9

One generation shall commend Your works to another, and shall declare Your mighty acts. On the glorious splendor of Your majesty, and on Your wondrous works, I will meditate. They shall speak of the might of Your awesome deeds, and I will declare Your greatness. They shall pour forth the fame of Your abundant goodness and shall sing aloud of Your righteousness. The LORD is gracious and merciful, slow to anger and abounding in steadfast love. The LORD is good to all, and His mercy is over all that He has made.

Shelter

The teacher said, "He'll never amount to anything."

This isn't the punch line to a joke or a witty one-liner from a stiff-necked principal in a 1980s teen comedy. This was my dad's teacher. His first-grade teacher. And she was describing my dad's future to his parents. In first grade.

For better or worse, times have changed. Nowadays, my father would have been moved to a different class or a different school due to his poor performance. At the very least, the school's administration would have reprimanded the teacher for her "honesty." But in the late 1960s, a teacher's pronouncement was gospel, and my dad was held back a grade.

If the first-grade version of my dad had heard the words used to describe God in Psalm 145, he wouldn't have had the slightest clue what the psalm was referring to. Slow to anger? Abounding in love? Merciful? That wasn't like anyone my dad knew—especially not the teacher who had told him he was nothing and would be nothing.

Just months after this parent-teacher conference, my dad was diagnosed with hearing loss due to a buildup of fluid in his eardrum. His hearing loss was so severe that, unbeknownst to his parents, he had been reading lips to get by in school. What that first-grade teacher had interpreted as ignorance and ineptitude turned out to be a practical problem, and one that could be solved. After the fluid was drained, my dad started to show significant improvement in school. This continued through high school, and by the time he was a junior, he had become interested in chemistry and had his sights set on a career in medicine.

As my dad began to sort out his future, his parents were trying to sort out their own. My grandpa's income was unstable, and his financial problems were taking a toll on his marriage. The decision was made to move to more-affordable housing. That was a good, responsible thing to do, but it meant moving my dad to a different high school for his last two years.

The move wasn't necessarily a surprise. Instability was the norm for the family at this point. They'd jumped from apartment to apartment every couple of years. What was upsetting about this move was leaving the place they'd lived for the past year: a house. My dad had never lived in a house before, and when his family was finally able to afford one, he was thrilled. It was a luxury to come home and feel safe—to go to bed at night listening to silence instead of the obnoxious next-door neighbors. So when it came time to uproot his life once again, my dad wasn't surprised—just disappointed.

And then, out of nowhere: compassion. Or as David says it, "The LORD is good to all, and His mercy is over all that He has made."

In my dad's case, goodness and mercy came in the form of his Aunt Shirley. Shirley and her husband offered to house my dad and his sister so they could finish high school at their familiar school. They'd stay with Shirley during the week and with their parents on the weekends, which would allow my grandparents time to work on their finances as well as their marriage.

And so this strange living arrangement turned out to be exactly what my dad needed. Shirley's son, Jay, was just a couple of years younger than my dad, and the two were already close friends. It made all the difference to come home and talk to a good friend as opposed to coming back to the chaos of an unsteady home. It was such a comfort to have a consistent meal on the table, a warm bed. It changed my dad's world to have the stability of a shelter from the whirlwinds of life.

Compassion changed my dad's world.

It's no wonder David gushes of God's goodness, justice, and mercy. When life gives you junk, treats you like junk, and tells you you're junk, a little compassion goes a long way.

In Revelation, John dreams of this same relief from the torment of life for the people of God: "Therefore they are before the throne of God, and serve Him day and night in His temple; and He who sits on the throne will shelter them with His presence. They shall hunger no more, neither thirst anymore; the sun shall not strike them, nor any scorching heat. For the Lamb in the midst of the throne will be their shepherd, and He will guide them to springs of living water, and God will wipe away every tear from their eyes" (7:15–18).

The compassion of my aunt and her family never left my father's memory. I don't know if he ever thanked them or repaid them for their generosity, but he certainly paid it forward. For as long as I can remember, my dad has had a heart for the homeless, and my parents' home is ever evidence of it. My godfather needed a place to live when he decided to go back to college, and my dad set up a room for him in our basement. My parents adopted my youngest sister. My grandma started living in their house several years ago. Even now, they don't hesitate to take in one of my friends when they need a warm bed and a hot meal.

My parents understand that when the world says you'll never amount to anything, God is still good. God demonstrated the fullness of His compassion in His Son's life, death, and resurrection. Jesus lived a life that shows us a way out of the storm of hate and violence. He died to shelter us from our own sin. And He rose to shade us from the shadow of death itself. It's those acts of mercy that give hope and give way to John's dream of a life without hunger, a life without thirst, a life without injustice—a life in God's shelter.

In the meantime, He gives us the tools and the means and the experience and the mercy to make a little shelter for those who need refuge.

As my dad will testify, a little compassion can change someone's world.

A little shelter can go a long way.

It's no wonder David gushes of God's goodness, justice, and mercy. When life gives you junk, treats you like junk, and tells you you're junk, a little compassion goes a long way.

Prayer: Lord God, Your mercy extends throughout all generations. Thank You for Your love and grace that You have showed to me and my family, and help me to extend the praise of Your righteousness in Christ to those who need the shelter of Your love. In Jesus' name. Amen.

DAILY STUDY QUESTIONS
Psalm 145:4–9

1. Think of a time when you felt absolutely safe and secure, and contrast that with a time when you felt threatened and imperiled. What are the key elements in creating a safe and secure harbor in an unsettled world?

2. How have God's actions in your life, His "wondrous works," provided you with what you need to experience security and safety?

3. When was the last time that you meditated? According to David, what are some legitimate objects of worthy meditation (v. 5)?

4. Why is the message of verse 8 a necessary and important elaboration on the declaration of verse 6?

5. David is quite certain that "men shall speak of the might of [God's] awesome deeds" (v. 6). In which contexts or settings do you think it would be inappropriate for a man to "eagerly utter the memory of [God's] abundant goodness"?

Psalm 145:10–13

> All Your works shall give thanks to You, O LORD, and all Your
> saints shall bless You! They shall speak of the glory of Your
> kingdom and tell of Your power, to make known to the children
> of man Your mighty deeds, and the glorious splendor of Your
> kingdom. Your kingdom is an everlasting kingdom, and Your do-
> minion endures throughout all generations. [The LORD is faithful
> in all His words and kind in all His works.]

Share the Love

Being a people of democracy, we have a tough time comprehending the king-dom concept. Even modern Great Britain, although it has a monarchy, is still governed by Parliament, not the solitary rule of its well-revered, beloved queen.

So when David speaks of *God's* kingdom, the analogy is a little lost on us.

As Americans, we're born with an innate distaste for this system of rule. That's precisely the sort of government our forefathers broke away from as they established their new nation. So it's easy to see why we're boggled by Jesus' adaptation of David's kingdom language.

Jesus spends a lot of time using this metaphor of a kingdom. The reason this sort of language was so evocative, so intrinsically electric, had to do with the context of the Jews' history and their plight at the time. For God's people, a people that came from a long line of less-than-loving rulers, a loving and *good* king was their dream—especially as they had been under the rule of the Roman Empire for some time.

Different Jews had different ideas about what the kingdom of Israel would look like once God returned power to His people. But as they turned their attention to Jesus, a man some said to be a messenger of God, they heard a message that focused not on Israel's kingdom, but on God's kingdom—the kingdom of heaven.

"The kingdom of heaven is like a merchant in search of fine pearls, who, on finding one pearl of great value, went and sold all that he had and bought it" (Matthew 13:45).

As opposed to the Jews' idea of a kingdom that overthrows Rome with power and might, or even of a kingdom that aligns itself with Rome as an ally, Jesus proposed a more enigmatic kingdom. This Kingdom is rare. It's hard to find. And perhaps most intriguing of all, it has intrinsic value.

You see, the man who sold all he had to buy the pearl is now poor. He has no money, and his only possession is the pearl itself. He might sell it in order to provide for his family, but then he wouldn't possess the treasure he sought in the first place. The pearl's only value is in the possession of the pearl—and nothing more.

So it goes with the kingdom of heaven, according to Jesus. Its value is in its possession.

My dad was fifteen when he began his search for fine pearls, and his questions started at Jewish summer camp.

Maybe I should back up.

My father's parents were raised Jewish, but they decided to raise their kids outside the faith. Not in another faith, just outside of the religion their parents had pushed upon them. They believed a person's faith to be a personal matter.

The benefit of my grandparents' laissez-faire attitude toward religion is definitely debatable, but this outsider's perspective caused my dad to raise questions about life. "Are we alone in the universe? Is there something more to this? If there's more than one religion, is there more than one God?"

And so here he was at the one summer camp his family could afford—not a Jew, not a Christian, not anything. He was just a sixteen-year-old boy trying to sort out the intricacies and mysteries of mortality. As it turned out, Jewish summer camp was just the place for these kinds of queries. Many nights were spent around a campfire, looking up at the stars, wondering what it all means. Others had similar questions, but questions were more prominent than answers.

My dad left camp frustrated as well as motivated to dig deeper.

As he continued to seek out answers to his questions, he found "This Is the Life," a family drama produced by Lutheran Hour Ministries that gave Christian solutions to contemporary moral problems. Every Sunday, my dad woke up to a new adventure with the Fisher family, a new Christian answer to the moral quandaries of life, and a step closer to some answers of his own.

By the time my dad made it to college, this TV show had made him familiar with the Christian language, and my dad felt comfortable speaking to Mike Phillips, a senior at his college. Mike happened to be a Bible study leader on campus, and he was willing to sit with my dad over lunch, over coffee, between classes—all to tackle some of my dad's questions. He didn't promise to have easy answers; he was just there as a friend, a human being, a fellow journeyman through life.

Before long, my dad felt like he had enough answers. Or maybe he felt like the answers weren't the important part anymore. Either way, he was welcomed into the Christian Church, and it changed everything. It changed the way he acted. It changed the way he dealt with people. It changed the way he looked at life—and he couldn't help but gush over this newfound way of looking at the world.

He began to write home, talking about God and Jesus and all that salvation stuff. But he wasn't just writing to his mom and dad. He was writing to his cousin Jay. He was writing to his other aunts and uncles. My dad expected controversy. He expected backlash from his Jewish relatives. But instead, he received . . . nothing. No response.

His religious conversion was never mentioned in his extended family. It was never questioned. It was never affirmed. It was never debated. In fact, he began to lose touch with his extended family. In part, this infrequent contact must have been due to the busyness of life, but my dad couldn't help but think it was because of his newfound belief system.

My dad quickly learned that the value of the Kingdom was in its possession. There were no fringe benefits. There were no external rewards. Life didn't get any easier. The world didn't turn black and white overnight.

But that didn't change my father's new point of view. He couldn't shake this new knowledge of God's faithfulness to His promises. He couldn't ignore the love of God toward all He had made.

It wasn't very long before all that introspection, all that soul-searching, turned inside out and manifested itself in loving concern for others: students on campus, my dad's family, his professors, and eventually my mom. In fact, his parents, the people who thought faith was a personal matter and nothing more, came to faith in Christ after my father shared with them what he had learned.

And that's the wonder of the parable of the pearl, isn't it? Like the merchant in the story, my dad had put his stake in the kingdom of God at great cost. He didn't want to trade it for some other good. He couldn't sell his newfound gift for profit. There was only one thing left to do:

Share the love.

As opposed to the Jews' idea of a kingdom . . . Jesus proposed a more enigmatic kingdom. This kingdom is rare. It's hard to find. And perhaps most intriguing of all, it has intrinsic value.

Prayer: Dear God, I praise You rightly when I declare Your great works for me and all Your creation. Help me to focus on Your greatest work—securing my salvation through Jesus—and enable me by Your Spirit to share Your love with others. In Jesus' name. Amen.

Wednesday

DAILY STUDY QUESTIONS
Psalm 145:10-13

1. What would be the pros and cons of living as a subject in an absolute monarchy?

2. When did you begin living as a subject of God's eternal kingdom?

3. What are the benefits of living long in God's kingdom? Are there any advantages for a person who is welcomed into God's kingdom later in life?

4. How do the King's actions in verse 14 contrast with what we normally expect of earthly rulers?

5. In what sense is it true that the "eyes of all look to [God]" (v. 15)? How do you make certain that *your* eyes look to God for your sustenance?

Psalm 145:14–17

The LORD upholds all who are falling and raises up all who are bowed down. The eyes of all look to You, and You give them their food in due season. You open Your hand; You satisfy the desire of every living thing. The LORD is righteous in all His ways and kind in all His works.

Sympathy for the Sick

My dad's call to Christianity created some unexpected changes in his life, not the least of which was his change in college major—a year before graduation.

For three years he had been a chemistry major. My father wasn't sure what to do with a chemistry degree; he had simply found out that he did well in the subject and fell into the major. But as he continued to read the Bible, he learned more and more about this God who cared for the oppressed.

It was a characteristic that connected with my dad. His whole life, he'd felt like he'd always been working against the odds, fighting to earn everything he owned, and here was the all-powerful Instigator of all things being described as one who "upholds *all* who are falling" and who "satisf[ies] the desire of *every* living thing."

And so my dad's heart was moved to serve the falling . . . quite literally.

I remember going to chiropractor school with my dad. He worked two jobs to provide for our family as well as the people he wanted to serve: anyone who had fallen or been in a car accident or had any kind of back and neck problems. But deep down, his heart really went out to those who couldn't afford the kind of quality care that, as my dad saw it, everybody deserves.

After all, everybody falls.

Before long, my dad was a chiropractic doctor working in an office alongside another doctor—a doctor nicknamed "Doc." Doc wasn't a Christian, was three times divorced, and yet, he had everything.

Cars. Friends. Big house. Traveled around the world.

This was another side to the health industry my dad hadn't seen before. He expected to be well off as a doctor, but Doc was more than well off. He was wealthy.

My dad was a man of God, trying to make ends meet for his wife and children, trying to help those in need—and Doc, this man of the world and man of himself, was being shown endless favor and given anything he desired.

A strange feeling filled my father. It wasn't exactly anger or jealousy, but perhaps it was spite. Or at least that's what the rush of emotion eventually became as his own measure of injustice ate away at him like the slow onset of influenza.

Like the subtle sting of infection.

Like a sickness.

In any case, my dad's practice continued to grow to the point that he was able to leave Doc's office and open an office of his own. I remember going to the office on opening day. My mom had made chips and salsa to welcome new patients, and the temptation was too much for me. To this day, the smell of salsa reminds me of that day and the unhealthy amount of tomatillo I consumed.

All-you-can-eat salsa was just the first of lifestyle changes for my family over the coming months. We moved to the suburbs. We moved into a bigger house. It wasn't a mansion, but a two-story.

My parents were judicious with their spending, but if there was one vice they couldn't resist, it was the temptation to spend money on their kids. Christmas Day was obscene: four kids climbing through piles and piles of wrapping paper and presents and stockings and toys. No present forgotten. No wish left unfulfilled.

Life was good, but I'll never forget the day that all changed.

It was a completely normal summer day. I had managed to get out of mowing the lawn (again), so it was my dad who was working in the backyard and I was in the living room when the doorbell rang.

As I walked to the front door, I began to recite my speech to whichever solicitation might be waiting on the other side: "We've bought our cookies this year. We have plenty of knives. We already have an encyclopedia set—it's called the Internet."

But when I opened the door, there was no badge-littered Girl Scout or pimple-faced college student-to-be waiting for me.

It was two police officers. They were looking for my dad.

This didn't take me completely by surprise. My dad's office served a community in the city where it wasn't unusual for a patient to be the victim (or instigator) of a crime. But as I looked into the backyard through our living room window, the officers weren't jotting down my dad's helpful testimony for their investigation. They weren't asking him to confirm a patient's injury.

They were handcuffing him.

Over the coming weeks and months, many people said many awful things about my dad. Some of these things were written in newspapers and heard on television, but those that stung worst were the things spoken in quiet corners.

Words of condemnation. Words of speculation over what he did or did not do.

And through all of this, I felt a rainbow of emotions. Anger. Despair. Frustration. But the most unexpected feeling was one of sympathy. I knew my dad's story, and I couldn't help but see life from his perspective. The kind of sympathy I'm talking about did not presume my father to be innocent, but, regardless of his guilt, understood and assumed the burden of his plight. By no good deed of my own, I felt some generosity.

Jesus attempted to explain this feeling to the Pharisees who questioned His association with selfish, thieving tax collectors—a group of people despised by the religious leaders. He said, "Those who are well have no need of a physician, but those who are sick. . . . I came not to call the righteous, but sinners" (Matthew 9:12–13).

And so goes God's generosity. He is generous to a fault. Yes, He gives food to the hungry. He gives shelter to the homeless, of course. But even more remarkably, He gives good to the bad, justice to the unjust, and love to the unloving.

Why?

He has come for the sick, not the righteous. The sick can be anyone, but as the Pharisees found out, it's often those who are most difficult to love. For the Pharisees it was the tax collectors. For my dad, it was the more-successful physician with questionable morals.

Regardless of whom we find it difficult to love, the truth strikes like a disease. We're all subject to sin and in need of grace. We all come up short. We all need compassion.

Because even the righteous do wrong.

Even the most upright fall.

Even doctors get sick.

And so goes God's generosity. He is generous to a fault. Yes, He gives food to the hungry. He gives shelter to the homeless, of course. But even more remarkably, He gives good to the bad, justice to the unjust, and love to the unloving.

Prayer: Dear Lord, everything good comes from Your fatherly hand. Pick me up when I fall, and treat me according to Your overflowing goodness in Christ, my Lord. I ask this in His name. Amen.

Thursday

DAILY STUDY QUESTIONS
Psalm 145:14–17

1. What's the most unsettling or disappointing "fall" that you have had the sad experiencing of witnessing firsthand? What lesson(s) do you take away from this experience?

2. Why is it both difficult yet imperative that we each come to terms with the reality that *everyone* falls?

3. What does it mean to have God "near" you (v. 18)? How might some see this as something less than comforting?

4. David asserts great and comforting promises in verses 18 and 19, but what restrictions does he place on these promises? Why is it that people seem to ignore these limits?

5. What difference will God's promise to *keep* you make for how you live the day ahead?

Psalm 145:18–21

> The LORD is near to all who call on Him, to all who call on
> Him in truth. He fulfills the desire of those who fear Him; He
> also hears their cry and saves them. The LORD preserves all who
> love Him, but all the wicked He will destroy. My mouth will
> speak the praise of the LORD, and let all flesh bless His holy
> name forever and ever.

Cry

Slam! Click. Click. Click. Click. Click.

This is jail. And that was the sound of the prison guard walking away. My dad didn't know when he would return, and, unfortunately, for the second time in less than two years, my dad began the first day of an indefinite stay in jail.

My father had already spent six months in jail for a crime he openly admitted he committed. He paid the price for his mistakes and had time to reflect upon his wrongs, but he wasn't allowed to return home after his release. After living with a friend for a few months, he returned to jail after refusing to confess to a different accusation—one he did not commit.

The circumstance before him was an intolerable ultimatum: either admit to a crime he didn't commit and eventually be released, or stand his ground and live behind jail bars.

He didn't know what to do, and his struggle with God was as complicated as the legal situation he faced. My dad writes: "I continued to plead with God and, from the depth of my soul and from every cell of my body, I wanted to be a godly man, husband, and father. I couldn't see His plan . . . if He even had one. I wanted it my way. I was stripped of everything I cared about: family, friends, possessions, home, profession, and now I felt like I had been stripped of God as well.

"I was not suicidal, I just didn't want to live."

My dad was face-to-face with misery, and in its terrible face, he cried.

Seeing my dad cry annoys me. I've never been able to explain it, but anytime I see him tear up during a particularly moving sermon, or on one of his kids' graduation days, or even during a chick flick, I'm filled with an overwhelming sense of irritation. It's the same kind of irritation you feel when you hear Paris Hilton talk about how difficult her day-to-day life is, or the kind of irritation you feel when someone at a TV station messes up and accidentally plays the same infomercial twice in a row. I can't explain why I don't want to see the same ad about the latest surround-sound alarm clock again, but that's the same feeling that washes over me when my dad performs that most unmanly of actions.

Because to me, *that* is not what a godly man is supposed to be like. Being a man means being like David: wake up, have a cup of black coffee, read *Blessed Is the Man*, pray, and go kill some Philistines. Right?

I mean, when David praises, like in Psalm 145, we feel the God-given manliness radiating from the text as if it were meant to be read by James Earl Jones:

"I will extol You, my God and King" (v. 1).

"On Your wondrous works, I will meditate" (v. 5).

"Your kingdom is an everlasting kingdom, and Your dominion endures throughout all generations" (v. 13).

That's what I'm talking about. I imagine David saying those words just before decapitating the general of an enemy army. "Your dominion endures throughout all generations" and *thwack*! Off with his head!

Yeah. *That's* a man.

But definitely not that pathetic, presumed-guilty man curled up in a jail cell, about to meet his self-imposed sentence.

The cell door opened and my father was led down a series of corridors before entering the courtroom. As he was placed before the judge, he hung his head in the face of judgment. This was it. He had already been called guilty; the only question remaining was, how long?

Seven years? Twelve years? Eighteen?

My dad would miss my wedding. He would miss all of my siblings' high school graduations. He might even miss the first birthdays of grandchildren that might come in the future.

As these thoughts swirled in his head, the judge looked up to pronounce the sentence. But it wasn't a number that came off his lips—just two words.

"Go home."

I'm sure there were more than two words involved, but those were the only ones that mattered, because those were the words that changed my dad's life forever.

My dad was overwhelmed. He returned to his cell to await his release and danced and shouted and sang and cried. But this time, the cries were cries of joy.

He was free. After one year, two months, and three days, my dad was going home.

David explores the idea of praise throughout the Psalms, especially in Psalm 145. Our instinct is to think of him as the strong, victorious king, confidently shouting his unending worship and praise to his almighty God—a kind of praise I can't exactly relate to.

At my best, my praise isn't that kind of praise. At my best, I rarely utter words of praise at all. If I ever praise God, it's more often at my worst than at my best. And in my worst, those shouts of praise are short of poetry. They're jumbled pleas for help and screams of relief and yelps of pain, and I rarely sing out the way I imagine David did.

I don't sing out. I cry out.

But that's the real beauty of the Gospel. Not that God takes us at our best—which He could—but what makes His love unconditional is that He takes us just as vigorously and enthusiastically at our worst.

At my worst, my prayers say, "If I have to choose between hell and You, I'll take You." My prayer is an insult to God and hardly worthy of being described as prayer at all.

Still, He takes our flawed prayers. He works through our broken actions. He accepts our cries as though they were praise. And we know that God accepts our cries, because He sent His Son to feel the pain of being human on earth where He was driven to a death so terrible that it caused Him to cry, "My God, My God—why have You forsaken Me?"

Jesus felt forgotten. Jesus knew what it was like to feel separated from God. He stayed on that cross, and though we rarely stay on ours, He somehow still understands our cries.

That's grace. Not that we praise God for His goodness, but that by Christ's victory over sin and death, our praise is called "praise" in the first place.

So as you go about your day-to-day life, may you see the Etch A Sketch® signs of

God's love. May His compassion give you shelter. May you share the joy of the Kingdom and find value in its possession. May God give you sympathy for the sick, and may your pathetic, imperfect, unwilling, regretful, pain-stricken, endlessly flawed cry praise His holy name forever and ever.

And that sound that you hear? It's the sound of your footsteps, because God has set you free.

But that's the real beauty of the Gospel. Not that God takes us at our best—which He could—but what makes His love unconditional is that He takes us just as vigorously and enthusiastically at our worst.

Prayer: Dear God, I'm unworthy even for You to come near me. But You sent Your Son, Jesus, to take on my human flesh so that I might participate in the blessings of His divine nature. Thank You, and accept my humble praise for Your undeserved mercy. In Jesus' name. Amen.

Friday

DAILY STUDY QUESTIONS
Psalm 145:18–21

1. When you think of praising God, do you think of poetry and singing or of agony and shouts of pain?

2. How can this wider understanding of what it means to praise God liberate and enhance your prayer life?

3. David emphasizes that his *mouth* praises God. Why might it be a good idea for Christians more frequently to speak their praise out loud rather than merely think it or pray it silently?

4. What does David accomplish in the final verse by speaking first about his own praise of God and then about the praise offered by "all flesh"?

5. The praise of God, David declares, will be universal in its scope, including all flesh, and eternal in its extent, continuing forever and ever. What does this teach about the nature of the eternal kingdom that God has promised?

Week Five

Psalm 145

The 145th psalm is a psalm of thanks for the kingdom of Christ, which was to come. It strongly urges the high, exalted work of praising God and glorifying His power and kingdom. For Christ's kingdom and power are hidden under the cross. If the cross were not extolled through preaching, teaching, and confession, who could have ever thought of it, to say nothing of knowing it? But such is His kingdom and power, that He aided the fallen, called the needy to Himself, made sinners godly, and brought the dead to life. Yes, He is the one who gives food to all, who hears the call of His saints, does what they desire, and protects them.

—Martin Luther

GROUP BIBLE STUDY
(Questions and answers on pp. 219–222.)

1. What are some of the specific, tangible things that God has done for you in the last week that rightly should move you to praise Him?

2. In the first verse, David declares his praise to God and then names Him "King." What does this title convey about God and about our relationship with Him?

3. What does verse 4 teach us about the content of our praise? How might this sort of praising of God differ from a typical understanding of what it means to praise God?

4. How does verse 8 provide not only a stirring motivation to praise, but also profound insight into the true greatness and glory of God? What evidence of this definition of God's character have you witnessed lately?

5. Why might this psalm put such a strong emphasis on the idea of God as king and we as subjects of His kingdom? How can this psalm's (actually, the whole Bible's) emphasis on monarchic images be made relevant to people infatuated with the leveling equality of democracy?

Blessed Is the Man © 2009 Concordia Publishing House. Reproduced by permission.

6. Many will recognize verses 15–16 as a table prayer, one that was suggested and encouraged by Luther. What is the significance of God having an open hand? How should this image encourage His people to pray?

7. David makes some rather bold and extensive assertions about what God will do for His people (vv. 18–20). He is near. He fulfills desires. He saves. He keeps. Given the extent of these promises, what kind of life should Christians expect to live? What shadow appears in these verses? What hint of what David expects from life?

8. Is the second part of verse 20 somehow out of place in this psalm, or is it a necessary aspect of the reasons that creatures have to praise God? What is the basis for your answer?

9. This is the last psalm of David to appear in the Psalter. What about this psalm makes it a fitting conclusion to David's collection of songs, petitions, and praises? How does the psalm have a personal yet more universal and inclusive appeal? What does this teach us about the ways that we praise God?

10. What concrete and specific changes can you make in your own prayer life to better reflect what you have learned about praise through your study of this psalm?

Week Six

Psalm 148

¹ Praise the LORD! Praise the LORD from the heavens;
praise Him in the heights!

² Praise Him, all His angels;
praise Him, all His hosts!

³ Praise Him, sun and moon,
praise Him, all you shining stars!

⁴ Praise Him, you highest heavens,
and you waters above the heavens!

⁵ Let them praise the name of the LORD!
For He commanded and they were created.

⁶ And He established them forever and ever;
He gave a decree, and it shall not pass away.

⁷ Praise the LORD from the earth,
you great sea creatures and all deeps,

⁸ fire and hail, snow and mist,
stormy wind fulfilling His word!

⁹ Mountains and all hills,
fruit trees and all cedars!

¹⁰ Beasts and all livestock,
creeping things and flying birds!

¹¹ Kings of the earth and all peoples,
princes and all rulers of the earth!

¹² Young men and maidens together,
old men and children!

¹³ Let them praise the name of the LORD,
for His name alone is exalted;
His majesty is above earth and heaven.

¹⁴ He has raised up a horn for His people,
praise for all His saints,
for the people of Israel who are near to Him.
Praise the LORD!

Jeff Williams

Psalm 148:1–3

> Praise the LORD! Praise the LORD from the heavens; praise
> Him in the heights! Praise Him, all His angels; praise Him, all
> His hosts! Praise Him, sun and moon, praise Him, all you shin-
> ing stars!

Responding to His Holiness

Psalm 148 is a psalm of worship. It begins and ends with praise. The imagery invoked is sublime and exalted. In the psalm, all that is celestial and terrestrial, in-animate and animate, is called to praise. The psalm is an invitation to all of God's creation—His angels and hosts, the sun and the moon, the heavens, the waters, the beasts and the trees, and the people of the earth—to praise Him. Obviously, lacking vocal cords, inanimate objects cannot praise Him, and animals and plants cannot praise Him like we do. Even the angels and hosts of heaven do not need a command to praise. They inherently manifest praise to the Holy One. The psalm is not primarily a list of commands directed to the elements of creation. It is rather an invitation, and for we who have been brought to faith, it is an outpouring from the heart of one redeemed, of a recipient of God's gracious provision, in worship to the holy and almighty God.

When I came to Christ many years ago, it was after several months of searching the Scriptures with the goal of understanding who He was. Although considered a pretty good guy and successful in all of the usual measures, my sin had all but de-stroyed my marriage and shattered my arrogance of pride and self-sufficiency. Some new acquaintances suggested Christ was the answer. It sounded promising, but I didn't want to jump on some religious bandwagon out of an emotional response. I did not want to "accept" Christ not knowing who He was and why. With what I now know was a providential trust in the Scriptures, I began my search, initially focusing on the Gospel of John and the Letter to the Romans, and then expanding to other books of both the Old and New Testaments. After nearly four months of daily study, the redemptive plan of God—initiated at creation and climaxing with Christ on the cross—began to come into focus. Also becoming clear was an intense and growing awareness of His holiness and my contrasting moral bankruptcy. By God's grace, I came to faith, trusting in Jesus Christ as Savior and the Lord whom I desired to please and obey; I realized the promised new life; and I embarked in an entirely new direction with new priorities. Our marriage and all other aspects of life experienced a wondrous restoration. As promised in Ephesians 4:22–24, I "put off [my] old self," and a transformation of the *mind* occurred. Scripture promises a new moral capability that the mind apart from Christ can never achieve—we are promised the *mind of Christ*, and all by grace. Being faithful to our gracious God continues to be my heart's desire, but my finite mind still struggles to comprehend the magnitude and significance of His holiness. Even after twenty years of growing to know God through His Word, I long to reach the place the composer of Psalm 148 gives testimony to.

To praise the Lord—or to simply say "Hallelujah!"—is to worship Yahweh. The worship is a joyful and grateful response to who He is and what He has done. In many Bible translations, *Yahweh* is translated as "Lord." It is the special name of God revealed to Moses in the burning bush in Exodus 3:14–15. God said to Moses, "I AM WHO I AM." And He said, "Say this to the people of Israel, 'The Lord, the God of your fathers, the God of Abraham, the God of Isaac, and the God of Jacob, has sent me to you.' This is My name forever, and thus I am to be remembered throughout all generations.'" "I AM" is the covenant name of God. God repeatedly uses this revealed name in the Book of Isaiah; for example, He says, "Listen to Me, O Jacob, and Israel, whom I called! I am He; I am the first, and I am the last" (48:12). And in John 8:24, Jesus (or *Yeshua*, which means "Yahweh saves") makes a direct claim of deity by taking the same name: "I told you that you would die in your sins, for unless you believe that I am He you will die in your sins." Here, Christ takes the name that reveals His eternal existence and His holiness.

Holiness is difficult to fathom. In our progressive world, we tend to relegate holiness to the abstract and the distant. Through the witness of Isaiah, we get a glimpse of holiness. In Isaiah 6, the prophet comes before the throne of the Lord, high and lifted up, and encounters the holiness of His character. The seraphim proclaim in verse 3, "Holy, holy, holy is the Lord of hosts; the whole earth is full of His glory!" Isaiah's response in verse 5 is absolute conviction of unworthiness in the presence of holiness: "Woe is me! For I am lost; for I am a man of unclean lips, and I dwell in the midst of a people of unclean lips; for my eyes have seen the King, the Lord of hosts!" Isaiah knows he cannot pass judgment. He pronounces himself as good as dead. He knows that because of sin, no one can see God and live. God's righteousness and holiness cannot allow it—that is, not without mercy and a gracious provision. And God grants that grace to Isaiah through the means of a burning coal (v. 7): "Behold, this has touched your lips; your guilt is taken away, and your sin atoned for." The burning coal on Isaiah's lips was a work of God—an external illustration of an internal cleansing—and a preparation for service. He came before God in all His holiness, fell broken and bankrupt, was purified, prepared, and restored, and was sent for God's redemptive purpose.

God is infinitely holy. He is enthroned on high. No sin can be in His presence. No sinner can stand in His presence unless granted grace—given that which is undeserved—and mercy—not given that which is deserved. Trusting in the promised redemptive work to come, the psalmist was a recipient of God's grace and mercy. Trusting in the redemptive work found in Christ, we are recipients of God's grace and mercy, through the gift of faith. Through faith in His atoning work on the cross, we are redeemed and our guilt is taken away. We are cleansed, given a new spirit, and enabled to glimpse the holiness of God. Our proper response is an ever-growing sense of gratitude and worship. Like the composer of Psalm 148, we grow to not only know and appreciate the gift of salvation, but the Giver Himself. In reading the psalm, we see not the psalmist, but the Lord worthy of praise and worship. And like the psalmist, our life becomes a proclamation of a redeemed worshiper before God in all His holiness. Let us praise the Lord!

....

Like the composer of Psalm 148, we grow to not only know and appreciate the gift of salvation, but the Giver Himself. In reading the psalm, we see not the psalmist, but the Lord worthy of praise and worship.

Prayer: Dear God, You indeed are worthy of my praise. Forgive me of my sins, and for the sake of Your Son, Jesus Christ, accept the praise of my lips and of my life as I seek to order my words and deeds according to Your Word. In Jesus' name. Amen.

....

Monday

DAILY STUDY QUESTIONS
Psalm 148:1–3

1. What are some things that move you to marvel and wonder merely by the fact of their existence?

2. Even if He had done nothing for you, why is God worthy of praise just by virtue of His sheer being?

3. It is true that literally *singing* praises requires a larynx, something lacking in many of God's created works. How might a wider understanding of *praise* expand the "praise choir" to include even these voiceless members of creation?

4. What is the relationship between offering praise and realizing blessings? Which comes first?

5. How is your praise life right now? When was the last time you praised God simply for who God is?

Psalm 148:4-6

> Praise Him, you highest heavens, and you waters above the heavens! Let them praise the name of the LORD! For He commanded and they were created. And He established them forever and ever; He gave a decree, and it shall not pass away.

Recognizing His Creative Power

The first reason the psalmist gives for his worship of the Lord is God's work as the Creator—Creator of all things in view and beyond view. For the psalmist, creation reveals, serves, and glorifies God. As John writes in Revelation 4:11 that God is "Worthy . . . to receive glory and honor and power" for His work of creation, so the psalmist summons all of creation to praise Him who made it. Calling all things— animate and inanimate—to praise the Lord is to say that all those created things give testimony to Him and invoke the praise due Him. That is a theme throughout the Scriptures. The testimony of the Word of God and the response of the psalmist in worship here first acknowledge the glory of God reflected in creation and proclaim His power demonstrated in it.

Ever since I was a boy, and long before I was familiar with the Bible and the story of redemption, the theories of evolution and related matters taught in school invoked a sense of skepticism and doubt. That life spontaneously self-started in simple forms and progressed to the diverse and complex forms we see around us made no sense to me. The theory that man further evolved so as to have self-awareness and to come to the place of considering such questions of beginnings made it even more mythlike. And, as I grew older and was introduced to the creation account in Genesis, the same sense of skepticism came along with it. Growing up with a strong interest in science and a curiosity about how things worked and why, I thought a miraculous and *unnatural* formation of the heavens, the earth, and all things was beyond explanation.

I now know why. By our very [fallen] nature, we rebel against the clear testimony of creation. In Romans 1:19–20, Paul writes of our rebellion in suppressing the truth of the Creator: "For what can be known about God is plain to them, because

God has shown it to them. For His invisible attributes, namely, His eternal power and divine nature, have been clearly perceived, ever since the creation of the world, in the things that have been made. So they are without excuse." Paul further writes that although we think ourselves wise in denying creation—and, hence, the Creator—we are actually fools in doing so. And our foolishness condemns us. Initially, that pronouncement was very offensive to me. Even after coming to Christ, I didn't take the account of creation literally, but considered it some kind of allegory. But as I further appropriated the substance of the Scriptures and saw its incredible internal consistency, I became convicted of its inherent truthfulness and saw my error.

Redemption found in Christ is accompanied by a new view of the world around us. Instead of denying the Creator in our deadness, we are given a new life with eyes to see and ears to hear. As Psalm 19:1 testifies, creation "declare[s] the glory of God, and . . . proclaims His handiwork." By grace we see His glory and hear creation's proclamation. We come to see that God's creative work is awesome and does invoke praise. It reveals to us His wisdom. Our appreciation of it is reflexive; that is, we appreciate its beauty, harmony, and order. That very appreciation gives evidence that we bear the image of God. Through faith in Christ, we see the world as resulting not by chance over time, but as a supernatural and miraculous work. "By faith we understand that the universe was created by the word of God, so that what is seen was not made out of things that are visible" (Hebrews 11:3). Whether standing at the edge of the Grand Canyon or a spectacular waterfall, or viewing the earth from an airplane or even a spacecraft in orbit, by faith we see God's work. We exclaim with the psalmist, "O Lord, how manifold are Your works! In wisdom have You made them all; the earth is full of Your creatures" (104:24). In that work, we see a tremendous order and harmony across the range of scale—from the atomic to the cosmic. We see goodness ("God saw that it was good" [Genesis 1:10, 12, 18, 21, 25]) and experience delight. Because God is restoring His image in us through faith in His Son, we see His work as an artist and a master craftsman. In gratitude for God's grace given to us, we share the perspective of Psalm 8, that all of creation is "the work of [His] fingers" (v. 3). And as we continue to study and appropriate the truth of God's Word, we grow in our understanding of the majesty of our Redeemer, even as the Creator Himself. For as Paul writes, "For by Him [Christ Jesus] all things were created, in heaven and on earth, visible and invisible, whether thrones or dominions or rulers or authorities—all things were created through Him and for Him" (Colossians 1:16).

The composer of Psalm 148 affirms that all of the creative work before us was by "decree" (v. 6). God spoke it—that is, commanded it—into existence (Genesis 1). Psalm 33:6 affirms that "By the word of the Lord the heavens were made, and by the breath of His mouth all their host." It continues in verse 9: "For He spoke, and it came to be; He commanded, and it stood firm." These passages speak of purpose. God, from eternity past, purposed a plan to be fulfilled in time. It started with creation, is progressively unfolded in the Old Testament, and culminates in the New Testament in the person and work of Jesus Christ. The writer to the Hebrews states it this way in the opening verses: "Long ago, at many times and in many ways, God spoke to our fathers by the prophets, but in these last days He has spoken to us by His Son, whom He appointed the heir of all things, through whom also He created the world" (1:1–2).

So Psalm 148 calls us to worship the Lord who is the Creator, and it proclaims that all of creation joins in the testimony of Him and gives praise to Him. All of creation serves His purposes in redemptive history to give Him praise and glory. In our fallen state, we are unable to acknowledge God as Creator, let alone show Him praise for creation. Although Ecclesiastes 12:1 commands us to "Remember also your Creator in the days of your youth," we cannot. In that unjust state of rebellion against Him, we deserve His just and eternal wrath. But in Christ, He grants us *mercy*, sparing us from the eternal separation and wrath due us, and gives us *grace*, endowing us with eternal fellowship with Him. Because of that grace and mercy, and indeed, by grace, we, too, can call all that is around us to praise—to praise Him who made it. Let us do so, in prayer and in how we live our lives, to our Creator.

....

Psalm 148 calls us to worship the Lord who is the Creator and proclaims that all of creation joins in the testimony of Him and gives praise to Him. All of creation serves His purposes in redemptive history to give Him praise and glory.

Prayer: Lord God, when I consider the work of Your hands, I am overwhelmed with wonder and awe. Thank You for putting me here at this time and place, and help me to spend my time on earth wisely so that others may come to know of Your redeeming grace. I ask this in Jesus' name. Amen.

....

DAILY STUDY QUESTIONS
Psalm 148:4–6

1. Is the doctrine of divine creation—in contrast to the idea of an undirected and nonsupernatural process of evolution—a source of comfort or a source of concern for you?

2. How does an orthodox Christian look at created things differently than one who dismisses God as an active force in creation?

3. What does verse 5 teach you about the authority and power of God?

4. What, do you think, is the "decree . . . [that] shall not pass away" mentioned in verse 6?

5. How does knowing that God has ordered creation and that it operates according to His will and decree affect how you think about the natural world around you? Do you need to change any attitudes or behaviors?

Psalm 148:7–12

> Praise the LORD from the earth, you great sea creatures and all deeps, fire and hail, snow and mist, stormy wind fulfilling His word! Mountains and all hills, fruit trees and all cedars! Beasts and all livestock, creeping things and flying birds! Kings of the earth and all peoples, princes and all rulers of the earth! Young men and maidens together, old men and children!

Acknowledging His Providence

Beyond creation and the beginning of time, the psalmist acknowledges a common theme of the Bible. This theme is all but overlooked in our day—that is, the providential working of God in His creation to bring His purposes to pass in time. We tend to forget or ignore that God is actively working throughout unfolding history and we attribute the outworking of our lives to chance, luck, and our own cleverness. But as verse 8 acknowledges, even the wind blows in "fulfilling His word!" *Providence*—a historic and somewhat archaic word—refers to God's governing of all the details of His creation and to any and all provision given. All of the biblical narrative assumes God's providential direction in redemptive history. And the composer of Psalm 148 not only acknowledges God as Creator, he assumes God's active involvement as Sustainer and Provider, and he responds in praise for that sustenance and provision.

When I came to faith in Christ more than twenty years ago, it was with a strong desire—indeed, a need—to be accountable, to submit to His lordship, and to grow in obedience to Him. According to Ezekiel 36:26–27, by grace, He had given me a new heart of flesh with a new inclination empowered by the Spirit toward the things of the Spirit of God. His Word promised victory over sin and growth in sanctification over time, and that by grace. In fact, in continuous reading and study of the Bible, I discovered an endless list of promises given, and all by grace. Those promises meant nothing if they were just promises without fulfillment. If they were truly promises, they would become manifest. And they have been made manifest and they continue to be fulfilled, in wondrous and incredible ways—not according to my desires and wants or what I thought best, but according to His wise purpose. In all those instances, the grace of God has made the promise, and the providence of God has fulfilled it. I have grown to recognize, acknowledge, meditate on, and thank God for His providences.

According to the Scriptures, there are several ways that God's providential work unfolds. At its fundamental level, providence sustains or upholds all of creation and preserves physical life. Paul tells the Colossians that Christ Jesus "is before all things, and in Him all things hold together" (1:17). The writer to the Hebrews proclaims that Christ "upholds the universe by the word of His power" (1:3). All of life is evidence of God's provision. Psalm 104 is full of acknowledgements of His providential hand in meeting the needs of His creatures. There, the psalmist writes: "You [God] make springs gush forth . . . they give drink" (vv. 10–11); "You cause the grass to grow . . . and plants . . . [to] bring forth food" (v. 14); "[God] made the moon to mark the seasons" (v. 19). He writes in words that portray all sustenance as a measure of God's outworking of grace. All creatures "look to You, to give them their food in due season. When You give it to them, they gather it up; when You open Your hand, they are filled with good things. When You hide Your face, they are dismayed; when You take away their breath, they die and return to their dust. When You send forth Your Spirit, they are created, and You renew the face of the ground" (vv. 27–30).

The imagery of providence and God's government supersedes the most powerful of man and even "brings the counsel of the nations to nothing" (Psalm 33:10). Proverbs 16:9 says that although man may plan his way, "the LORD establishes his steps." In Proverbs 21:1, Solomon writes, "The king's heart is a stream of water in the hand of the LORD; He turns it wherever He will." And in a special and specific way, the providence of God is at work in bringing His chosen to faith. Paul writes in Ephesians 1:4 that "He chose us in Him before the foundation of the world, that we should be holy and blameless before Him." In John 10:27–28, the Good Shepherd testifies to His providential call and keeping of the sheep of His pasture: "My sheep hear My voice, and I know them, and they follow Me. I give them eternal life, and they will never perish, and no one will snatch them out of My hand." Providence further preserves us (Psalm 37:1–8), protects us (Psalm 91:4), and leads and guides us (Psalm 23:2–3). All the products of providence are to both our temporal and eternal benefit. They are the execution of God's decrees and the fulfillment of His Word. In testimony to the efficacy of His Word and the fulfillment of God's providential purposes, Isaiah 55:9–11 records:

For as the heavens are higher than the earth, so are
My ways higher than your ways and My thoughts than your
thoughts. For as the rain and the snow come down from heaven
and do not return there but water the earth, making it bring
forth and sprout, giving seed to the sower and bread to the
eater, so shall My word be that goes out from My mouth; it
shall not return to Me empty, but it shall accomplish that
which I purpose, and shall succeed in the thing for which
I sent it.

Paul further encourages us in Romans 8:28 in regard to the provision of God's ways: "And we know that for those who love God all things work together for good, for those who are called according to His purpose."

But sometimes, providence brings us difficulties. Those times may be consequences of sin and come for our chastening (Hebrews 12:5–12); they may come for our strengthening (2 Corinthians 12:7–10; 1 Peter 5:10); to give opportunity for God's comfort and grace (2 Corinthians 1:3–7); or they may come for no discernible reason at all (Job; John 9:1–3; Romans 11:33–36). What is our proper response to these truths? We are to go to the Scriptures for the answer. "Trust in the Lord with all your heart, and do not lean on your own understanding. In all your ways acknowledge Him, and He will make straight your paths" (Proverbs 3:5–6).

The teaching of God's providence in governing and providing for all of His creation and, in particular, His children has become among my most treasured. Understanding, acknowledging, and trusting in God's providence brings us closer to the perspective of the psalmists in praising the Lord, our Sustainer and Provider. Through Christ and by His grace, we have a relationship with our Lord. God's providential care is the means that He engages in that relationship by extending care to us in temporal matters. In a healthy relationship, we acknowledge and appreciate the love and care of another and seek to reciprocate with a similar love. In the same way, our acknowledging and appreciating the love and care God expresses to us in providence stimulates us to love Him in faithful obedience to His Word. In response, our relationship expands and deepens. And we can appropriate the words, in prayer, of Psalm 33:20–22: "Our soul waits for the Lord; He is our help and our shield. For our heart is glad in Him, because we trust in His holy name. Let Your steadfast love, O Lord, be upon us, even as we hope in You."

According to the Scriptures, there are several ways that God's providential work unfolds. At its fundamental level, providence sustains or upholds all of creation and preserves physical life.

Prayer: Lord God, You deserve praise from everything You have created, both the seen and the unseen. Forgive me for my shallow thinking, Lord, and help me to see with fresh eyes Your providential care in my life and in the lives of those I love. I ask this in Jesus' name. Amen.

Wednesday

DAILY STUDY QUESTIONS
Psalm 148:7-12

1. Thinking about your own life, what evidence can you see of God's providential hand caring for your physical as well as spiritual needs?

2. Why do you think people tend to be more impressed with God's providential care when it is direct and "miraculous" than when He works in ordinary ways within the regular workings of the created realm?

3. What method is used for ordering the list of earth's creatures that are exhorted to praise God? How does the psalmist's orderly progression through the different realms of earth increase the sense of God's providence through creation?

4. Why are "great sea creatures" the first creatures named when the psalmist turns his gaze from the heavens to the earth?

5. What makes the message of verse 11 exceedingly relevant even in our world that only knows royalty as mascots or souvenirs of a bygone era?

Psalm 148:13

Let them praise the name of the LORD, for His name alone is
exalted; His majesty is above earth and heaven.

Living Out Our Vocation

As we consider and meditate on Psalm 148 and consider its exhortations for
our Creator, Sustainer, and Provider in the context of all of Scripture, we see an exalted perspective of the Lord in His holiness. "His name alone is exalted; His majesty is
above [all]!" Those words of praise and the entire psalm also reveal something of the
psalmist before Him. We see the composer of the psalm as a child of God, a recipient
of God's grace and provision, and a subject of God's rule. But more than that, we see
in the psalm a *response* from God's child, God's chosen, and God's subject. We see a
response of praise overflowing with gratitude and with a transcending disposition
of contentment. That contentment transcends and is independent of circumstances.
Getting to a place of true contentment—as manifest in the outpouring of the psalmist—can be an elusive challenge for us in life. The means to meet that challenge, like
all challenges of life, can be found in the Bible.

It was very early in my Christian walk when I began to marvel at the whole
concept of true contentment and the varying degrees to which it was manifest in the
lives of people around me. We all admire those people who always seem to be in a
settled and contented place, regardless of what life brings their way. We also know
of those who usually are very discontented in life, no matter what good things come
to them. We usually enjoy the company of the former and avoid the latter. Contentment usually can be observed alongside a disposition of gratitude. Contentment
also comes with humility and a general transparency of life. In a similar way, discontent often comes with ingratitude, self-centeredness, and little transparency.

In Philippians 4:11–13, Paul gives witness to true contentment:

Not that I am speaking of being in need, for I have learned
in whatever situation I am to be content. I know how to be
brought low, and I know how to abound. In any and every

circumstance, I have learned the secret of facing plenty and hunger, abundance and need. I can do all things through Him who strengthens me.

Long ago, several aspects of Paul's witness became obvious to me. First, Paul had *learned* contentment, and that meant that I could too. The Bible teaches us to acknowledge God's hand in all things, to submit to God's providential care, and to seek to honor Him in our response. It teaches us to see things with an eternal perspective instead of in time. It continues to teach us of the grace of God. All of that teaches us contentment. The second thing I noticed was that Paul wrote these things while in chains, imprisoned in Rome. Before coming to Christ, my degree of contentment was directly proportional to my circumstances. Here, I saw contentment *independent of* circumstances. Not only that, but Paul's sense of contentment did not waver with want or abundance. He not only had a contentment that could not be diminished with less, but could not be increased with more. It truly transcended circumstances. Given the very challenging circumstances in which we can all find ourselves in life, I yearned for a state of contentment that would be transcendent—one that could weather the storms of life *and* one that I would not take for granted in times of plenty. Third, Paul's contentment came with a strong expression of gratitude. In spite of being in chains, Paul was grateful for the care and concern of others. He was grateful to God. His expression of gratitude gave witness to his contentment. Finally, Paul's contentment gave him the strength and power to withstand and endure *all things.* Not only had he by the grace of God gained the state of contentment, but that state was the source of his strength. In a related way, Paul considered his life as a calling—a divine calling—so he saw all things as the outworking of God's providence for a purpose. God's purpose was above and beyond Paul, and Paul was to rise to that purpose. It is a basic principle that we, in Christ, are to be content to serve Him in the positions He has placed us. In his response to that calling—or vocation—Paul and the psalmist are examples to us.

For me, experiencing contentment that transcends circumstances has always been proportional to my degree of understanding what I call "the offices of life" as callings from our gracious God. Whether it is husband or parent, soldier or astronaut, Bible teacher, carpenter, or home gardener, all those roles and tasks of life are vocations for which I have been summoned by God. Even in the midst of the most difficult circumstances, I have found that in viewing those "offices of life" as vocations, I can trust that they are from our wise God, that He has given me the provision and discernment to meet their challenges whatever the circumstances, and that His wise purpose will be fulfilled in my obedience and faithful response. Furthermore,

I consider it an honor to do so. In a very real way, in our proper response to God's callings—our vocations—we find the *Christian life.* Approaching all of life's roles and tasks in this way rightly brings contentment because it is an outworking of a proper relationship with the Call Giver. Contentment presupposes a relationship between the Creator and the creature, the Provider and the one provided for, the Redeemer and the redeemed. It is a relationship that confirms the contentment found in Psalm 37, particularly verses 4–5: "Delight yourself in the LORD, and He will give you the desires of your heart. Commit your way to the LORD; trust in Him, and He will act." Not that He will give us all of our desires, but our true desires will more and more conform to His as we delight in Him, trust in Him, and commit our ways to His ways in obedience.

In Psalm 148, as in much of the Bible, contentment is evident as God is exalted and the author is diminished. We realize that contentment comes as we begin to see God's providential care in the callings of life and our response to those callings. True contentment, a grace gift from God, transcends our circumstances. Prayerfully meditating on this teaching of the Bible relieves us of stress, worry, and discontent. It is a promise that brings rest and comfort to the troubled soul. And it frees us to be like the composer of Psalm 148 in exalting the "His name alone," Jesus Christ, and proclaiming "His majesty" above all.

....

Approaching all of life's roles and tasks in this way rightly brings contentment because it is an outworking of a proper relationship with the Call Giver. Contentment presupposes a relationship between the Creator and the creature, the Provider and the one provided for, the Redeemer and the redeemed.

Prayer: Lord Jesus Christ, thank You for calling me to the different vocations in my life in which I may serve others in love. Bless my wife, children, employer, colleagues, and friends, and help me to fulfill my tasks to the best of my ability, trusting in Your grace. In Your name I pray. Amen.

....

Thursday

DAILY STUDY QUESTIONS
Psalm 148:13

1. Why do genuine praise and contentment always accompany each other? Which is the prerequisite for the other . . . or are they simultaneous?

2. How much do *you* need to be content?

3. Suppose someone is trying to learn contentment. What's the most important thing for him to do—or is contentment a personality thing that can't be learned?

4. What's the difference between praising the Lord and praising His name?

5. In what sense is it true that the entire psalm was building up to the last line of verse 13? In the day to come, how will you answer the invitation to praise this great God?

Psalm 148:14

He has raised up a horn for His people, praise for all
His saints, for the people of Israel who are near to Him.
Praise the LORD!

Praising Him for His Redemptive Work

This week, as we have worked our way through Psalm 148, we have considered the response of the psalmist that comes before the holiness of the Lord, the glory of the Creator found in His creation, and God's providential sustaining and ordering. We have also considered the delight, gratitude, and contentment evident in the psalmist. The reason behind the psalmist's praises and his evident disposition before the Lord comes to a focal point in verse 14. It is fair to assume that the composer of the psalm is an Israelite, and that he is among the "people of Israel," and that those people are the ones who are "near" to the Lord. This is where it gets very personal. The psalmist not only sees and proclaims the glory of the Lord, but he is "near" Him and in relationship with Him!

This climax in Psalm 148 was the same climax I came to years ago in my search to understand who Jesus was, why He was so significant in history, and why He could turn my life around. Up until then, the Psalms didn't mean a lot to me. They were simply the words of a dreamer without substance. But once I saw Christ's work on the cross as the focus of all of history, understood the spiritual significance of that event, and came to the realization that my newfound sight and understanding were entirely the work of God by grace, the Psalms came alive, and I joined the psalmist in his response. Now, as David proclaims in Psalm 119:103, God's words are "sweeter than honey to my mouth!"

The composer of Psalm 148 comes to a crescendo in the proclamation that the Lord has "raised up a horn for His people." A horn was a symbol of strength and prosperity—especially of a nation. The context, in the Old Testament history of Israel, recalls the reigns of David and Solomon and looks forward to the promised return to those days of glory. The context in redemptive history recalls the promises of God made throughout the progressive Old Testament revelation and looks forward to the anticipated fulfillment of those promises. It looks back to the promised Messiah and forward to the fulfillment in Christ. This is where we see Christ in Psalm 148! David praised the Lord in a similar context in Psalm 18:2, where he wrote, "The LORD is my rock and my fortress and my deliverer, my God, my rock, in whom I take refuge, my shield, and the horn of my salvation, my stronghold." Luke 2 is the very familiar passage recording the birth of Christ that is often read to us on Christmas. Just before that, there is a passage perhaps not as familiar. In the latter part of chapter 1, Zacharias, the father of Jesus' cousin John the Baptist, prophesied something wondrous in response to a vision and the naming of John. Zacharias proclaims in verses 68–69, "Blessed be the LORD God of Israel, for He has visited and redeemed His people and has raised up *a horn of salvation* for us in the house of His servant David." Zacharias goes on to proclaim the fulfillment of the promise of salvation—a covenant promise first given to Abraham—and a Savior, the "horn of salvation." Zacharias referred not to his son, John, but "someone greater than [he]" (John 1:26–27). That someone was Jesus, the Christ.

The psalmist anticipates Jesus Christ in the reference to the horn "raised up" and also the favor of the Lord manifested in the provision found in Christ. The horn was raised *by* God *for* people—a people *near* to Him. This reference to a personal relationship is also found in a like way in Isaiah 43:20–21: "I . . . give drink to *My chosen people*, the people whom I formed for Myself that they might declare My praise." And in Psalm 135:4, the author proclaims that "The LORD has chosen Jacob for Himself, Israel *as His own possession*." Two critical things stand out in these Scriptures. First, the possessive pronouns emphasize that the people are *His*, and He claims them as *His own* and the ones *chosen by Him*. These words reflect God's perspective. He considers Himself in a personal relationship with them. And the second critical element of this context is that the relationship is solely initiated by and is the result of God. The people are completely passive in being drawn into the court of the King, as it were. The Lord—on His own initiative and in spite of their sinfulness—chooses them, brings them into His presence, and calls them His own. The Lord does so in a way the psalmist doesn't anticipate—through the cross.

The cross is the manifestation of God's love to a people to be called His own. There is nothing inherent in those chosen that draws His love. His love is unconditional and volitional. It is a perfect love that pays the ultimate price that His holiness requires. God is infinitely holy and just. His justice cannot leave sin unpunished. His holiness will not allow sin in His presence. We are sinful and inclined toward evil. Our due justice is death. Jesus Christ was given to suffer and die in our stead. He was without sin and took our sin upon Himself, with the provision of satisfying the justice of God and redeeming us from our due. That is the ultimate manifestation of love. He convicts us of our sin, offers us the provision found in Christ's work, brings us to repentance, gifts us with a faith that trusts in that provision, and causes a rebirth of a new person, with a new inclination toward the things of God. That provision comes with the perfection and righteousness of Christ, credited to us. It is a great and wondrous exchange. God places our sin on Christ and places His righteousness on us (2 Corinthians 5:21). And that gift is for eternity! It is the inexpressible gift Paul referred to in 2 Corinthians 9:15. It is the gift of grace that rightly causes a response, as in the composer of Psalm 148, of praise, wonder, gratitude, and obedience.

Our life should reflect that of the composer of Psalm 148 as we contemplate our God, ponder the significance of His provision, and grow in our relationship with Him—the relationship that He initiated. He uniquely created us, sustains and provides for us, and redeemed us to be His own. He, the Creator and Lord of the universe, takes on our humanity in order to be near us. How humbling it ought to be to be summoned into the court of the King and not only be allowed to live, but be given a place of honor—for eternity. What a gracious King we have. When we go before the Lord in prayer, let us respond like Paul: "Oh, the depth of the riches and wisdom and knowledge of God! How unsearchable are His judgments and how in-scrutable His ways!" (Romans 11:33). Praise the Lord!

....

He, the Creator and Lord of the universe, takes on our humanity in order to be near us. How humbling it ought to be to have been sum-moned into the court of the King and not only be allowed to live, but be given a place of honor—for eternity.

Prayer: Heavenly Father, You raised up Your horn of salvation, our Savior Jesus Christ, for me and all sinners. Even as You draw near me through Your Word, enable me to draw closer to those You place in my life, so that through my words and deeds, they may likewise praise Your name. For Jesus' sake. Amen.

....

Friday

DAILY STUDY QUESTIONS
Psalm 148:14

1. What have you done lately that should prompt God to love you?

2. How does it work? Do God's godly ones offer praise and then He lifts up a horn of salvation for them, or is it the other way around?

3. How has God lifted up a horn for you?

4. What does the incarnation of Christ have to do with your nearness to God?

5. In what sense is verse 14 the right climax to this litany of praise? How is "Praise the Lord!" the only imaginable ending?

Week Six

The 148th psalm is a psalm of thanks that ex-
cites and exhorts all creatures in heaven and
earth to praise God—especially His saints, the
children of Israel, who worship Him, that is,
have His Word and worship. And note that this
psalm confirms all the stations of life—kings,
judges, old, young. All are created by God and
are good and honorable. For if the office of
king or of judge were evil and not God-given,
one could not in such an office praise God. But
where there are kings and judges, there will
also be subjects, servants, hangmen, soldiers,
laborers, farmers, townspeople; where there
are young and old, there will be married people,
children, and household servants. All are honorable and good and show that their Creator is
good. Rightfully, all of creation should be nothing but a tongue, always praising this great
goodness of God. If you want to know how
good a thing is, then take whatever you will and
say: "If there were no fire . . ." or "If there were
no sun . . ."; "If there were no hangman . . .";
"If there were no woman . . ."; and so on. Then
you will see why one should thank God.

—Martin Luther

GROUP BIBLE STUDY
(Questions and answers on pp. 228–231.)

1. What are some of the largest worship gatherings in which you have participated? Which one was most meaningful to you? What was it like?

2. What plan or order seems to be directing the writer as he works his way through the list of creatures invited to join in the praise of God? What message does this structure convey to the reader?

3. One of the early Soviet cosmonauts infamously attacked belief in God by quipping from orbit that although he was traveling in the heavens, he had seen no sign of God. How might the psalmist respond to such a comment? How does a person's worldview affect what he sees?

4. As the psalmist compiles his invitation list, he includes many members of creation that "naturally" praise God (sun and moon, hills and trees) and others that praise Him by vocation (angels and heavenly hosts). Why does he exhort creatures to praise when they already do it without being told?

5. In verses 5 and 6, the psalmist makes a strong point about the origin of the many invisible and heavenly beings he has mentioned. Why does he need to stress that they were created by God with little more effort or energy than the speaking of a word? What sort of errors in the theology and thinking of twenty-first-century Christians might be prevented by a better grasp of this reality?

OKAY TO COPY THIS PAGE.

6. What does it mean that the "stormy wind" also fulfills God's Word? What word does it fulfill? How do we explain to people (to ourselves!?) that "natural disasters" caused by the stormy wind are actually fulfilling God's Word?

7. How different are the groups of people listed in verses 11 and 12? What is the one thing that has the potential to unite and bind them? What implications does this hold for interactions between different cultures and between competing nation states?

8. Verse 13 is explicit and unmistakable in its declaration: "His name alone is exalted." How much room does this leave for the idea that all religions are legitimate expressions of man's spirituality and are to be valued and respected as equally true? What about the idea that other religions simply have "other names" for the same God that we worship? How do we reconcile the need to be socially and culturally sensitive and tolerant with the need to be doctrinally and eternally truthful and faithful?

9. How does the climax of heavenly praise described in verse 6 differ from the climax of earthly praise related in verse 14? Why is it critical to recognize God's unilateral activity and creation's responsive receptivity as essential to the praise of heaven and earth?

10. How has this six-week study changed your understanding of what it means to praise God? In light of the truths you have contemplated in this study, what will you do differently?

Small-Group Leader Guide

This guide will help guide you discover the truths of God's Word. It is not, however, exhaustive, nor is it designed to be read aloud during your session.

1. Before you begin, spend some time in prayer, asking God to strengthen your faith through a study of His Word. The Scriptures were written so that we might believe in Jesus Christ and have life in His name (John 20:31). Also, pray for participants by name.

2. Before your meeting, review the session material, read the Bible passages, and answer the questions in the spaces provided. Your familiarity with the session will give you confidence as you lead the group.

3. As a courtesy to participants, begin and end each session on time.

4. Have a Bible dictionary or similar resource handy to look up difficult or unfamiliar names, words, and places. Ask participants to help you in this task. Be sure that each participant has a Bible and a study guide.

5. Ask for volunteers to read introductory paragraphs and Bible passages. A simple "Thank you" will encourage them to volunteer again.

6. See your role as a conversation facilitator rather than a lecturer. Don't be afraid to give participants time to answer questions. By name, thank each participant who answers; then invite other input. For example, you might say, "Thank you, Al. Would anyone else like to share?"

7. Now and then, summarize aloud what the group has learned by studying God's Word.

8. Remember that the questions provided are discussion starters. Allow participants to ask questions that relate to the session. However, keep discussions on track with the session.

9. Everyone is a learner! If you don't know the answer to a question, simply tell participants that you need time to look at more Scripture passages or to ask your pastor.

DAILY STUDY QUESTIONS

Monday   Psalm 40:1-3

1. While we might think immediately of trials and temptations that have been threatening us, the devotion rightly reminds us that the ultimate "slimy pit" is the grave. The deaths of family and friends bring us sadly and painfully near to the pit.

2. Thinking about death has a way of bringing all of life into sharp perspective. When we consider the grave, we are confronted with the one "pit" that should concern every man, and the one pit from which no man can ever rescue himself. This thought demands that we face that fact of our own desperate helplessness.

3. Patient waiting is the final definition of discipleship because the life of a believer—which is the life of a disciple—is always founded on the reality of a person's complete dependence on God for everything. Thus, busyness is in fact antithetical to the heart of Christian life. Until one learns to give up and wait patiently (wonderfully exemplified by the patience of a corpse!), he is resisting the work that God will accomplish.

4. The human spirit (especially as it is cultivated in the context of the "American spirit") dies a hard death and will find any possible excuse to maintain its own independence and sense of self-importance. One of the best excuses is the claim that God doesn't want us to be lazy and idle . . . a truism, but irrelevant when it comes to learning to wait patiently for God. Self-preservation prevents God's plan from unfolding. Preservation is the business of the Creator, not the creature.

5. David was quite sure that once he was rescued, the new song that he would inevitably sing would result in the conversion of those who would be unable to ignore the dramatic impact of the Lord in the life of one of His rescued people.

Tuesday   Psalm 40:4-5

1. Maybe it's top-grossing movies, top-rated golfers, top stocks, or fastest-growing churches in the nation—lists and "best of" rankings have a way of holding our interest.

2. No two lists will be the same. While we should all be grateful to God for some obvious common blessings (life, salvation, guidance), we all enjoy unique individual blessings from God that fill our lives with delightful gifts from His gracious hand.

3. Listing the wonders God has done for you goes a long way to helping you reaffirm the wisdom and blessing of placing your trust fully and only in Him. Realizing the extent of the gifts already given provides tangible reason to expect His continued giving—even when the desired good results are not immediately evident.

4. Surprisingly, for many people it is not the "Super Bowl" challenges (like life-threatening illness or sudden natural disaster) that pose the most severe threats. Rather, it is the ordinary stuff of life—trusting God to guide you through a conversation with your teenage son, trusting God and His ways when your co-workers' behavior demands a firm rebuke, counting on God to provide enough financial resources to get you through another month—these are the sorts of things that often tempt a man to stop trusting God and start trusting his own instincts . . . the deceitful instincts of a proud liar.

5. While we may hesitate to lump *all* people into the "proud liars" category, David does not hesitate to make the blanket assertion. Perhaps his hard experiences with proud liars had given him ample reason for this seemingly harsh position. Or, more likely, David was simply willing to be forthright about the reality of fallen man: he is always a proud liar. The choice *is* that simple: either trust God and be blessed or trust man and be burned.

Wednesday   Psalm 40:6-11

1. Whether it is a father sacrificing sleep for an infant or the last piece of dessert for a growing fifteen-year-old or a husband sacrificing his afternoon plans for the sake of his wife's agenda, we all make what we consider significant sacrifices. Of course, some of us will have made far greater sacrifices for the sake of others—sometimes for total strangers.

2. Because God has told us that we are to love our neighbors as ourselves, the truth is that God fully expects us to make just the sort of sacrifices as the ones you recalled in answering the first question.

3. The obvious answer is that the "I" is David, who wrote the psalm. Yet it is more profoundly true that the "I" is the one who went into the pit and then rose triumphantly from that pit: Jesus Christ, the true Davidic King and Messiah who does God's will and who fulfills God's purposes. For those who are now joined to Christ through faith, it is also true that they are each the "I" who now lives as Christ lived and who makes known His truth.

4. The one who does God's will makes God's reality known (v. 10). This is a sharp reminder for those who claim Christ today but seem unwilling or hesitant to

make His truth widely known. Yes, this is a stern reminder of the need to do the work of evangelism.

5. God's loving kindness is evident in the Gospel proclamation of the forgiveness of sins—undeserved and unmerited. But God's truth—not only the Gospel, but also His guiding and directing will for His creatures—also preserves. When we live in obedience to His will, we are able to avoid many dangers and sorrows. In other words, conformity to God's truth contributes to the preservation of life even now.

Thursday   Psalm 40:12-16

1. Sadly, most of us can probably readily recall more than one time when our sins caught up with us and we found ourselves in a sorry condition.

2. When we are overwhelmed by the sheer enormity of our failure, it is tempting to think that God cannot possibly still care or that there is any way possible to emerge from the wreckage of what you have done. This is precisely the sort of thing Satan wants you to think! Not only does the chaos of our sin obscure your ability to see God's grace, but it clouds your ability to see *anything* accurately. Sin distorts your vision of reality as you see everything in the context of what is twisted and perverted by its destructive power. Consider the sort of ridiculous things people do when caught in a chronic lifestyle of sin.

3. In a sense, verse 12 is the prerequisite for 13; only when we are so crushed by our sin that we despair of saving ourselves and die of "heart failure"—a failure to accomplish anything by sheer willpower or good intention—are we ready to admit our need for deliverance. This is the classic distinction between Law and Gospel.

4. It is God's glory, His very nature, to deliver His people, beginning with His delight in forgiving their sins for the sake of His Son, Jesus. There is wild comfort in the truth that God does not tire of His task and that He is, in fact, more willing to give mercy and forgiveness than we are ready to admit our sin and need.

5. David had a long history of waiting for God's promises to be fulfilled and had no doubt learned that one could depend on God to come through. But it may be that he had also learned something about God's timing; hence his appeal to God that He not delay. What creatures seem slow to learn, however, is that God will also use the discipline of waiting itself to accomplish His purposes in the lives of His people. Times of waiting can be remarkable times of growth.

Friday   Psalm 40:17

1. Athletes are not the only ones looking for blessings. And while the traditional Chinese blessings are typically high on most people's lists, we have other goals and blessings that we desire. These are not inherently bad or antithetical to the Christian life—indeed, they are often the very sorts of things that God also desires for us. The critical point, is to recognize the place of such blessings—they belong here, in this world, and in our interactions with other creatures. Before God, however, it is a different story altogether.

2. The point of the devotion is abundantly and painfully clear: God only blesses losers. This is fundamental truth. The beginning point for the Christian life is always the same. We all begin as broken, desperate losers who cannot help themselves. Utter, abject dependence on God is the place where we all must start. Winners don't need help. And before God, in the excruciatingly bright light of His holiness, no one is a winner. Only fools insist that they have what it takes. Only the self-deluded think that they can venture into God's presence with a swagger of confidence, ready to receive the blessings they have earned. God's blessing is never earned. It is freely given to losers.

3. Care must be taken not to pervert even the posture of helplessness and neediness into some sort of performance. In other words, being a loser is not an achievement. It is a reality that is forced on us in spite of ourselves. Not sought, it comes with irresistible compulsion. And it comes, always, as a result of a close brush with God and His holiness. God's standard is too high. It does us in. It leaves us dead. It declares us to be losers. To be brought low to the essential point of receptivity, simply consider God's expectations for your living. Think about His Law.

4. Not only does God deliver from sin, Satan, and death (Luther's unholy trio of woe), but He also delivers us from futility and meaninglessness in our present lives, from disease and suffering, from enemies bent on our destruction, and from raw fear bred by all of the above.

5. The content of the prayer would be impossible if David wondered—even in the smallest degree—about God's benevolence or His ability to provide the deliverance David needed. Only the strongest and most vital confession of faith is able to cling to God when the Creator determines that waiting and trials are the things that His people most need if they are to be the people He has created them to be.

GROUP BIBLE STUDY
(Questions are on pp. 40–41.)

1. *Think of a time when you had no choice but to wait patiently. What were the circumstances, and how did you handle the situation?*

Whether it was the failure of technology or the failure of our bodies, there are usually many circumstances that can force us to face the reality of our own complete inability and helplessness. Impatience and restlessness are typical reactions to such impositions on our agendas . . . and our autonomy.

2. *"Patient waiting" seems to be the definition of* good disciple. *Why might Christians have a hard time coming to terms with the requirement that they learn and even embrace such patient waiting?*

In the final analysis, patient waiting is an admission of personal failure, need, and helplessness—the very sorts of things American men have been taught to fear and fight and, when all else fails, deny. Even Christians possess a remarkable a capacity for prideful self-confidence, assuming that they don't *really* need any help.

3. *In Monday's devotion, the author confessed an increasing appreciation for the liturgy: "I realize it relieves me of finding the right things to say and sing. Instead, we give up our ideas and use the words God has given us for worship." What do you think about this idea? How can it be possible that the liturgy is a "new song"?*

Some might consider a discussion of the liturgy to be a loaded topic, but the author of the devotion is quite right to find comfort in singing and praying back to God the words that God has first given us. What makes the song new is not the originality of the tune or even the fresh poetic arrangement of the words, but the fact that it is a song not of human worth and accomplishment but a song of Gospel—a song that celebrates the reality of a God who raises us from death—the only really new thing that matters to dead creatures. Such celebration is the heart of the liturgy, whether sung with tunes written yesterday or twelve hundred years ago. (It might be worth noting that on one of their early albums [*War*, 1983], the Irish recording group U2 recorded a track titled *40*, which was simply a new—and, some would add, compelling—arrangement of the first verses of this psalm.)

4. *In verse 4, David asserts God's blessing for the man who "has made the LORD his trust." If faith is something the Holy Spirit must create in each of us (Ephesians 2:8–9), what does David mean by making man the one who does the choosing?*

This is another perfect example of theology's twofold nature. It *is* all about God and His sovereign choice. He must do the whole work of saving—including the work of creating faith in a human heart. Yet, simultaneously, God holds each man responsible for the choices he makes or fails to make, and faith in God is the expected work of every creature. David further reminds us that *we* daily make choices about the object of our trust. God grasps us through His powerful Word, and then we decide the extent to which we will rely upon Him and follow Him in our ordinary routine. To choose God's way, every day at every juncture, is to choose blessing.

5. *What does David mean in verse 6 when he asserts, "Sacrifice and meal offering You have not desired. . . . Burnt offering and sin offering You have not required," when, in fact, God had specifically required such sacrifices from His people? Is there a proper place for ritual or sacrifices in the lives of Christians?*

Verse 8 holds the key to understanding this apparent contradiction. David's not implying that sacrifice and obedience are mutually exclusive. Indeed, David himself did not fail to make the appointed sacrifices. Empty ritual—that is, ritual done for its own sake without recognition of the relationship with God that precedes and undergirds it—is wrong because it fosters ideas of self-sufficiency and merit. Interestingly, sheer obedience without awareness of the underlying relationship creates the same disgusting result. The whole point of the Old Testament sacrificial system was not a way of earning forgiveness but a means of cultivating the right relationship between God and man as sinful man learned to look to God for forgiveness and for the provision of every need. God is not interested in people using His gifts (whether sacrificial ritual or sincere obedience to the Law) as tools for leveraging their own justification. But both of these things are quite appropriate when done as aspects of a life of faith lived in dependence on God's grace.

6. *How does this psalm undergo a sort of metamorphosis from being simply praise to being stunningly messianic? Point out all the parts of the psalm that receive new meaning or significance when read in the context of Christ's life and mission.*

The delight in the mercy of God's saving action—extraction from the pit—is certainly cause for rejoicing, and it is an experience common to all believers. Somewhere around verse 7, however, one begins to get the impression that there is more going on here than simple praise. The one written about in the scroll of the book is best identified with our Lord Jesus, who in His ministry exemplifies virtually every verse of this psalm. Even the confession of sin (v. 12) can be related to Christ as we think of His final task as the sin-bearer on the road to Calvary.

7. *What is the relationship between sin and seeing (v. 12)? What implications might this truth have for society as well as for families and individuals?*

Sin not only condemns us before God, but it distorts our vision of reality. When we are caught in some sin, we do not see accurately; that is, we do not make good judgments about what is happening and about what we should do or not do. In other words, people who are caught in a sinful lifestyle tend to do stupid things. If sin obscures our vision and clouds our judgment, then it is no surprise that our society as a whole is incapable of solving perennial problems that beset our lives together. Not only do we not have the answers, but we cannot even rightly identify the real problems. There is certainly a wealth of possible contemporary examples that the group can offer as evidence of this truth. The implication, of course, is that without a mind-set driven by God's reality—one founded on forgiveness—it is impossible to rightly grasp the realty of the world around us. In other words, sinful man is in sorry shape, with no hope of saving himself or his society.

8. *What's the difference between seeking God and loving His salvation (v. 16)?*

Actually, at least as far as this verse is concerned, there is no difference. This is a good example of Hebrew parallelism. The second part of the verse simply reiterates the sentiment or idea of the first portion, but with different wording or vocabulary. This verse is not proof that the Bible endorses "seeker services." In this verse, the one who seeks God is the one who already believes and who desires to better know and follow; the seeker is also the one who loves God's salvation and praises Him accordingly.

9. *How are we able to read (much less pray!) verses 14 and 15 without cringing at words that sound embarrassingly self-serving and, well, . . . vengeful?*

Yet a third category of psalm now appears in this psalm of praise: the imprecatory prayer. David prays for the humiliation of his enemies. While it might seem that this is quite an egocentric petition, one needs to remember that in this case, David's enemies are God's enemies. David is God's chosen king; to thwart David is to run afoul of God's plan. So in these verses, David is praying for the triumph of God's truth over anything or anyone that is false and evil. To seek God's justice is necessarily to desire the defeat of evil—including those who refuse to repent of their evil. Christians, who bear the name of Christ and serve and speak in His stead, can also join David in praying for the overthrow of their enemies—even as we pray for their salvation. In the wisdom of God's truth, these are not mutually contradictory prayers.

10. *The last verse of the psalm captures the central theme of the entire psalm. What is the cause-and-effect relationship that seems to be at work in this verse? Why is the first part of this relationship so rarely heard or accepted?*

The appeal for the Lord to be mindful, to come to the rescue, is based on the fact of the psalmist being afflicted and needy. In other words, the prerequisite for God's action is human failure and helplessness. Capable and confident people are not in the position to pray for God's aid. This is a hard word, one that does not resonate in the climate of the twenty-first–century western world of self-sufficiency, pride, and "human dignity." Even in the Church, this message is often met with disbelief and resistance. People do not want to hear such a "depressing message." No doubt, emphasizing human failure and neediness is a hard sell, but it is the absolute requirement. Until we admit our emptiness and need, we cannot receive what God is eager to give.

DAILY STUDY QUESTIONS

Monday   Psalm 66:1-4

1. It may have been a live sporting event, an exciting game on TV, or some personal triumph, athletic or otherwise, that led to the spontaneous outburst. Perhaps the most genuine expressions of such joy go virtually unnoticed by the one who celebrates—they are simply natural and feel right.

2. Though the practice may not fit best in the context of Sunday's Divine Service, delighted outbursts of joy are perfectly fitting in your relationship with God. When you consciously recognize the role of God in the good you experience, it will be natural and right to speak His praise—altogether appropriate. An exquisite sunrise, a spectacular mountain vista, a personal triumph in business or on the athletic field, a favorable report from the doctor—all of these can well prompt a joyful shout.

3. In the context of Scripture, a reference to "all the earth" is best understood most naturally not as a reference to all people but to all of creation. The Bible often calls on the creation to acknowledge its Creator or points out the fact that the creation praises God more faithfully than does God's caretaker of creation: man. The creation offers its praise to God simply by doing what it was designed to do; it honors God by fulfilling His plan for it.

4. As people who remain sinful even as we profess faith, we may recognize in our own lives times when our obedience is more superficial and coerced than heartfelt and eager. While the external actions may be indistinguishable whether done from faith or from fear, the internal motives are quite different . . . and quite obvious to God. So it is that even our motives can become yet another stimulus to repentance and confession.

5. The creation praises the Creator by doing God's will for it. This is not a bad way to think about your own life of praise: you praise God best simply by doing what He created you to do. From this perspective, all of life becomes a song of praise to God.

Tuesday   Psalm 66:5-7

1. "Come and see" is quite direct. The psalmist invites the reader to consider the hard evidence—no doubt, he would even gladly walk with the reader to the edge of the Jordan, the very site of God's intervention, and then point to the people of Israel filling the land as the proof of God's loving work. It was not some spiritual

fulfillment or "otherworldly" reality that defined the psalmist's hope. It was tangible, material, and present. Such is God's way of working.

2. Perhaps such a journey would begin at the baptismal font and then continue to the communion rail. From there, it would no doubt take many different turns as each person tells the story of God's faithfulness to him in specific and concrete ways—ways that can often be seen and experienced even now. Of course, we recognize that the ultimate fulfillment of God's promises is yet to come, fully manifest only at the Last Day.

3. Whether such events are understood as merely luck, chance, circumstance, fate, demonic, or divine depends entirely on the point of view one has before the occurrence takes place. Faith learns to see God's preserving hand in all events (mundane as well as spectacular) and rejoices in God's good provision.

4. The God who keeps watch has no tolerance for rebellious self-exalters, and justice will be enacted. While it might seem like people get away with murder—and worse—no one escapes God's final reckoning of justice . . . no one. It seems that the sin that most offends God's holiness is human pride and absurd claims of self-sufficiency.

5. It may well be that our "Christian realism" sometimes slips into what more closely resembles skepticism than faith. Expecting great things of God—even material and tangible things—is the mark of one who sees clearly that God's hand directs all things. And even if our expectations are not immediately and completely fulfilled, our faith will continue unabashed since God's will is always best. Christians do expect great things from God, and they do keep trusting when those great things don't materialize according to their expectations.

Wednesday   Psalm 66:8–12

1. Perhaps you can't tell a cliff-hanger story, but given the realities of childhood and life in a broken world, odds are good that you have something close.

2. At the time of a close brush with death—whether real or imagined—people are often quite adamant about the valuable lessons they learned. It may well be true that lessons were learned at the time. But life's story and its frequently remarkable and dramatic episodes can provide even greater lessons when it is reviewed and reconsidered from other perspectives. What was once a lesson in obedience can become a lesson in God's care and the surprising ways that His plan can develop.

3. As always, the psalmist recognizes God's hand in all that he experiences. It is God who brings the affliction and God who makes sense of the trial. Indeed, "trial"

is exactly the right word since God uses the experience to try and to refine His people. This idea is consistent throughout the Scriptures, including the New Testament (Hebrews 12:6). This may call for some rethinking of cherished notions about what God will or will not do. To see suffering in the context of God's plan is to recognize that even what is evil is made to fit into God's immediate and ultimate purpose.

4. The point is that we may need to check our assumptions about what God has in mind. It may well be that one of God's children will not experience anything even remotely like a "place of abundance" in all of his years of life in this broken world. And for any Christian, the promise of the Christian life is only fully fulfilled at the day of resurrection. The real "place of abundance" for which we all yearn is the eschatological kingdom brought to reality at Christ's return. This means that we cannot claim this or other Scripture as proof of God's intention to bless us with wealth, health, prosperity, or happiness in this life.

5. Whatever the negative circumstances that are troubling you, when they are recognized as God's means of accomplishing His purpose in your life, your attitude toward them and toward God's activity in your life can be dramatically altered. This is the secret that St. Paul learned which enabled him to greet *all* of life's circumstances with an appreciation for God's purposes within it all (Philippians 4:10–14; 2 Corinthians 12:7–10).

Thursday   Psalm 66:13–15

1. Perhaps you recently married, joined a group with a pledge, had business in court, or signed a legal document. All of these amount to vows that you have made.

2. *If* we recognize that God has a stake in the fulfillment of every vow and promise, we may gain a greater appreciation of the importance of every vow and the need to insure that each is honored. In other words, they are all significant—from the vow of marriage to the offhand promise made to a child.

3. On at least one occasion, it seems that the psalmist had made a bargain with his God and was now seeing it through by fulfilling his part of the deal. While such deal making is not uncommon, its wisdom is dubious at best. Since God is already fully committed to our salvation and eternal prosperity, bargaining with Him is needless at best and dangerous at worst. It can easily and wrongly lead one to conclude that he somehow has leverage with God and actually *can* bargain with the Almighty! On the other hand, seeking God's aid and deliverance is always a good idea—especially when the "spot" you are in is particularly constraining.

4. To recall that you are going to God's house, the place where God is present for you, helps to keep the right perspective on the event. One can hardly overemphasize the wonder, reverence, and awe that should attend our attitude toward worship and the meeting that takes place there. Yet, this is also a pleasurable meeting, since, like the psalmist, we also enjoy an intimate relationship with our Host. We converse with Him—"*Your* house," not "the Lord's house."

5. *Vow* is a rather plastic term, enabling a multilevel application. We pay our "vows" to one another by honoring our commitments and keeping our word. We pay our "vows" to God by faithfully using the gifts He has given and making ourselves regular guests at His Supper. Ultimately, though, we don't pay any vows at all . . . they have all been fully paid already by the One who accomplishes all things for us. Our relationship with God is not about transactions and debt ledgers intended to keep the vows and their fulfillment square. It is about grace. Vow fulfillment belongs to the tasks of this life and your responsibilities to your fellow creatures.

Friday   Psalm 66:16–20

1. The fact that you are alive and able to read or hear this question is already potent evidence of God's blessing this day. Look around at your immediate setting and consider the Author and Provider of all that you have and see, and you will find yourself compiling a list that seems to be infinite. Fallen humans are incomprehensibly self-centered, greedy, impatient, and ungrateful beings—small wonder that we fail to see the blessings that surround us.

2. We tend to think of our witness in relation to nonbelievers. But the psalmist reminds us that we have a responsibility also to the family of the faithful, encouraging them with our words and deeds to rejoice with us in God's provision and to remember God's ways of dealing with us in mercy. This is, incidentally, a compelling reason for attendance at worship: your presence alone is an encouragement to other Christians in ways you may never appreciate.

3. The first half of the verse is about what we would expect from someone who is facing a tough situation, and in desperate need of help: he cries with his mouth! Indeed, crying is right. But the second half may seem a bit odd. Along with a petition for aid, the psalmist includes praise of God. Of course, this is not so surprising. A moment's reflection on God and His character should move any creature to praise, regardless of the circumstances. God is always worthy of our praise, even when we feel that life is closing in and the situation is desperate. When things are tough, seek God's help and sing God's praise. This is the example of the psalmist.

4. A wicked heart is the lot of us all. We are sinful by nature and by deed, and we are competent sinners at that. Scripture teaches us that this problem is not eradicated by achieving sinlessness, nor is it a matter of sincerity or purity of heart. (A pure and sincere heart is a standard far too steep for any human polluted by the corruption of sin.) No, this problem of sin blocking our avenue to God is dealt with in only one way: by repentance. Mercifully, this "requirement" is an option open to us all.

5. God's loving kindness (*chesed* in Hebrew) is His undeserved grace—which is always the fundamental reality when we have sinned. God owes us nothing, but gives us everything. The concrete evidence is His naming and claiming you at the font and His giving to you week after week in Holy Communion. The Means of Grace are all the evidence we need.

GROUP BIBLE STUDY
(Questions are on pp. 66–67.)

1. Can you recall a time when you experienced such a remarkable blessing or received such good news that you could not help telling even strangers what had happened? Tell the group about it.

Men have a well-deserved reputation for being tight-lipped about things . . . especially personal things . . . especially emotional, personal things. Nevertheless, in spite of our natural tendencies, there are those rare occasions when even the most silent male will be so overwhelmed with some great gift or blessing that he will find himself (often to his own personal amazement) volunteering the information to other people, even to people he does not know. While you have yet to undergo this phenomenon personally, you might be able to recall a time when you witnessed it in the life of another.

2. Since the whole earth is invited (commanded!?) to give praise to God, (vv. 1, 4), in what ways can a man seek to join his voice with a creationwide symphony rather than merely offer his own individual ditties?

This idea carries some significant implications. It is good and right to think of creation performing a splendid symphony in honor of its Creator simply by being the creation and doing what God designed it to do. Thus a man's highest praise may well be offered not on a Sunday morning, but all week long as he blends his "voice" with the voices of all creation, finding his fitting part within the symphony and playing it with zeal and joy. This is about finding and fulfilling the vocation(s) given to you by God. One's entire life, and not just the larynx, becomes the instrument of joyful praise.

3. How can you tell when someone comes cringing to God (v. 3)? What difference does it make?

Perceptivity not being a universal virtue among men, it may well be that we cannot distinguish between fake obedience and the real thing. A good hypocrite is impossible to spot—that's the point, after all. While this is likely, at least initially, to be upsetting, perhaps it doesn't matter that much as we live our lives in service to one another. God knows the truth; for us, it is enough to be doing and receiving the right things in relation to one another. Before God, it makes a significant difference, but as far as we are concerned, it matters little.

4. *The psalm celebrates God's mercy displayed in the dry water crossings of the exodus. What good does it do us to remember such ancient events? What is the purpose of these divine interventions?*

To recall and retell the story of God's faithfulness to His people emboldens us to trust His continued care for His people. God will care for His Israel . . . yes, also the new Israel, His Church. These ancient saving events should not be diminished as mere pointers of some greater reality yet to come. They are much more than symbols. Ask a dry-shod Israelite standing on the far shore of the Red Sea what the crossing symbolized and he would laugh in your face. The crossing *was* the gospel of God's intervention. It *symbolized* nothing! It is better to see these events as foretastes of the fuller reality that is yet to be revealed. Similarly, there much more than symbolism going on in our celebrations of the Lord's Supper, but this event of gospel itself is yet a foretaste of the greater banquet yet to be served at the Last Day. We are wise to receive material gifts of grace with gratitude and simplicity and not attempt to "baptize" them into some "greater" spiritual meaning.

5. *What kind of watch does God keep on the nations? How do you reconcile the reality of enormous evil at work in so many nations with a God who keeps watch?*

Reality screams loudly and we may well be tempted to conclude that while God is keeping an eye on things, that is about all He is doing! It is not easy to reconcile a caring and intervening God with nations that seem to act with indifference to His law and without any restraint imposed from on high. It is helpful in the face of such questions to remember that time is measured differently by God than it is by us, and justice that appears to be delayed or even nonexistent is, in God's reality (the only reality that finally matters), right on schedule and altogether thorough. We can find comfort in the knowledge that nothing is lost on our God, and justice will prevail against the nations that flout His will.

6. *Does the confident promise of verse 12 (and even the wonderful assurance of Romans 8:28) mean that we will always see good things happen if we simply continue to wait patiently and faithfully? How might it be possible for such thinking to become problematic or even dangerous?*

God will certainly fulfill His promise, but it must be understood that His definition of *good* may not agree with what most humans assume to be *good*. It is clear that God's good is the spiritual growth and salvation of His people. What it takes to accomplish those goals may not always translate into what we ordinarily consider to be good and pleasant experiences. To "claim God's promise" may lead some people to assume that in a year or so at most, God will work everything out, and the unpleasant circumstances of the present will resolve themselves into a wonderful future reality of blessed happiness. It is not uncommon for Christians to struggle mightily with the inconsistency between what they experience and what they assume God will do for them when He makes "all things work together for good." What is needed is a greater appreciation for the fact that God's good may demand some challenging and even painful circumstances.

7. What abrupt shift does the psalm makes in verse 13? (Pay attention to the first-person pronouns.) What do you think of this move? How does this shift shed light on the relationship between the individual and the congregation?

Remarkably, the psalmist who had been speaking with plural pronouns, acting as the voice of the whole congregation, now speaks in the singular, referring to himself and his own relationship with God. Rather than cutting out everyone else in an egocentric inward focus, however, the psalmist teaches the right relationship between the individual and the group—or, in this case, the nation. The individual does not lose himself in the group—as happens in a mob—but actually finds himself. Because of his relationship with God and with the community of believers, the individual actually more fully understands himself and his place within God's world. The Christian's bond with the body of the faithful does not strip him of his personhood or individuality, but brings both to their fulfillment.

8. Considering Jesus' stern counsel in Matthew 5:36–37, what's the difference between taking a vow, making a promise, agreeing to something, and merely giving tacit assent?

The typical response, of course, is to engage in an extended and nuanced debate about what exactly constitutes a vow, a promise, an agreement, and a consent by default and what makes each different. Jesus and Scripture, however, seem to be making a different point altogether: be a man of your word. Regardless of what the circumstances or the accoutrements may lend to the weight of a particular promise, from God's perspective, none of that matters. A passing yes to a child's idle request is no less important or binding on a Christian man than a legal vow made on the Bible and in front of thousands of witnesses. A promise is a promise, and a man of integrity keeps his word . . . no matter what.

9. Some would like to summarize the Christian faith with a handful of basic principles that, when kept, guarantee God's blessings: love God, love people, get blessed. Do you think this is what the psalmist meant in the last verses of this psalm? What's the problem with this sort of thinking? What would you say to someone who was promoting it?

God is neither a vending machine nor a cosmic bellhop waiting to do our bidding if we ask the right way, with the right heart, with the right credentials, or with the right capital (a stockpile of "good works" to be used as leverage). The desire to condense Christianity into a quid pro quo "game" designed to wrest blessings from God is a common, yet deadly, perversion of our faith. Indeed, it is insidious—second nature to us all—and requires unremitting vigilance if it is to be held at bay. The psalmist knows better than to play this game with God. It is idolatry as it inevitably creates a god that bears no resemblance to the One who actually reigns and directs our lives . . . including the timely delivery of blessings in spite of our performance. Those who teach such things need a firm rebuke and an invitation to return to biblical faith in a God who acts in grace and not in response to supposed merit.

10. *What vows need your renewed attention? What testimony do you need to give to fellow believers? What praise do you need to include in your routine petitions? In other words, what difference will this psalm and its message make in the way that you live in the days to come?*

God's Word does not exist only to be studied—it is the Spirit's tool to change its readers. God wants to change you with this psalm. Consider concrete and specific actions that should be evident in your living as a result of the Spirit's work in this portion of God's Word.

DAILY STUDY QUESTIONS

Monday   Psalm 116:1-4

1. Most of us can tell tales of "close calls," and some can even relate near-death experiences. Those without the benefit of such encounters have no doubt heard the firsthand accounts of others. While it would seem reasonable that brushing so near death would profoundly alter a man, the truth is that often, as the memory of the event dims, so does its impact on the person.

2. It is possible to read conditional love into this verse, but to do so would be to miss the point of the context. The psalmist has not arrived at a decision to love God because God came through for him in a pinch. Rather, in the afterglow of such a dramatic deliverance, the writer of the psalm simply bursts with delight: "I love You, God! You do such remarkable things. You even answer my prayers!" It is not so different from a child exuding: "I love you, Grandpa, because you give the best gifts!"

3. The psalm gives the sense of death and its close companion, Sheol (the general place of the dead in the Old Testament), as aggressive predators hunting victims to trap, entangle, terrorize, and destroy. Death is neither passive nor benign, but an active force of evil at work in the world. Too often our culture makes an uneasy truce with death by pretending that it is "just part of life" or that it is a friend to be greeted without fear, or by blunting its horror by naming it a mere datum of finite existence. The Old Testament, and this psalm, will have none of that. Death is a creeping, constant evil bent on your ultimate destruction.

4. When confronted with the terrifying reality of death, the psalmist has only one response; it is the only thing he can do: he turns to Yahweh and pleads for Him to save his life. This is exemplary as both the fitting response of faith (looking to God when the situation is desperate) and the theological reality that God is the one who is in control of even the frightening reality and is certainly able to save if He so chooses.

5. Obviously, the psalmist provides a stirring example of prayer with an economy of words. Mindless repetition of clichés, trite phrases, and familiar but threadbare wording all have a way of invading our prayers and weakening them by their overuse of words. Often the simple and short prayer is best: "O Lord, save my life."

Tuesday   Psalm 116:5-7

1. Childhood fears run the gamut, from illogical fantasies of monsters under the bed, to improbable terrors like burglars in the closet, to very real and all-too-common fears like humiliation at school or divorcing parents. As adults, our fears may be more sophisticated, complex, and numerous, but they are every bit as troubling and unwelcome during the day's final quiet moments.

2. That God is compassionate is a keystone of our faith, but it is hardly a given for many or even most religions in the world. It is a mark of Christian faith, then, to learn to see the evidence of God's compassion in the everyday events of ordinary life. Rehearsing some portion of those proofs is not only an encouragement for faith but a form of praise.

3. *Preserve* is a word rarely associated with caring for someone. *Preserve* is what you do with a bumper crop of blackberries, or what you try to do with perishable food. When it comes to preserving people, we probably think of cryogenics more readily than we think of compassionate intervention and the saving of lives. But when God preserves us, He is saving us, and He preserves us by sustaining us with His gifts and grace. Perhaps the best preservative God uses in our lives is the preservative of the Means of Grace that enliven and empower us for the routine of life and the crises of life.

4. The psalmist assumes that the ordinary state of things is a soul/heart (the inner "core" of a person) that is at peace with God, the world, and itself. Calamity or danger upsets this rightly ordered rest and is at odds with God's plan for man. This is an important thought because our contemporary culture seems to operate on the assumption that people are typically out of alignment with God, the world, and self—hence the insatiable appetite for therapy, self-help books, compensating pleasures, and Oprah. The idea that a person's status quo should be equanimity founded on right relationships with God and creation is an often-overlooked aspect of Christian faith.

5. Not merely *enough* or *adequately*, God deals with us in ways that are *bountiful*. He always goes to extremes in His giving and has no concept of rationing or stinginess. Our lives explode with the good of God's bounty—and that is never better demonstrated than in the abundant grace won and delivered in our Lord Jesus.

Wednesday   Psalm 116:8-14

1. Actually, this is quite a complicated issue. Ultimately, Christians readily confess that all that is good in them can only come from God and His mercy at work

through them. They take no credit for their successes. On the other hand, God holds each of us accountable for using what we have been given, and He fully expects us to accomplish much with the talents, opportunities, and resources that He has entrusted to each of us. Maybe the best way to handle this is to refuse to praise or congratulate yourself, even as you do your best to use every gift the Lord has given you in faith in Him and in loving service to your neighbor. This is the way that God has planned it to be, after all.

2. Because God has rescued the psalmist from death and kept his feet from stumbling, he is now able to walk before the Lord, not in Sheol, but in the land of the living. But the same words can be read as a promise; in joy for what the Lord has done for him, the psalmist commits himself to walking *before the Lord*, which has strong implications for the moral caliber and integrity that will now mark his way of life. These thoughts certainly are not mutually exclusive, and perhaps it is best to recognize both messages as correct and relevant.

3. To "walk before the Lord" means to walk fully exposed and fully accountable—before the Lord, nothing is hidden. If one is to walk in such a way, then, he is inviting God's continual oversight and consenting to God's judgment. Clearly such careful divine observation delivers more than a twinge of intimidation. Yet, one is also confident before God because He is a God of compassion, and so there is unspeakable comfort that settles around the one who has committed himself to walking continually in God's presence. There is no safer or more secure place for any man to walk than before God. Before the Lord, all is seen that is true; yet, before the Lord, all is also forgiven.

4. In the second half of verse 10, the psalmist laments that he feels crushed by his affliction; and in the next verse, his disillusionment over the broken state of creation reaches the extreme. Nevertheless, both of these painful and soul-rattling challenges are experienced in the context of faith. Even as a committed believer in God's compassion and grace, he yet undergoes the most dramatic trials and personal misgivings. The lesson is clear and critical: Faith does not remove the trials, nor do the trials eradicate faith. Rather, faith is proven by its ability to face squarely the hard realities of life and to handle them by seeking the only possible help: God's help.

5. To treat the question as merely rhetorical or theoretical is to miss the import of the query. The psalmist is in earnest about the question, and even apart from the worthy example he provides, the question itself is a powerful tool in teaching Christians the sort of attitude that should predominate in their thinking and acting. In light of "all His benefits," what *can* you give to the Lord? Be careful not to jump so quickly to the "right" answer—"Nothing! Jesus did it all; I just receive"—that you

fail to realize the positive impact such a perspective can have on your attitude and your way of living. It is worth considering the difference it might make if you began to live in intentional response to what God has done for you. Is it worth actually trying it to find out?

Thursday   Psalm 116:15–16

1. There are precious metals and precious gems, of course. There are even Precious Moments, though few men would give those intolerably cute, doe-eyed figurines much thought. Precious things are rare and costly. Many precious things are irreplaceable. The most precious things usually add the third component of emotional and relational significance that will permit no measurement of valuation. Precious is very much in the eyes of beholder.

2. The psalm is a celebration of the singer's rescue from the snares of death. In this psalm, death is clearly the enemy. Yet, in verse 15 we are told that what the Lord considers precious is a *death*. It would be easy to accept that the Lord considers His godly ones, His saints themselves, to be precious. But the psalmist says explicitly that it is the *deaths* of these godly ones that is precious. Clearly, it would be reasonable to us if what God considered precious was the rescue or salvation of His godly ones, but it is frankly odd to hear that what He thinks precious is the passing—the death—of His chosen, godly ones.

3. In this case, the key to interpretation is the way that one understands *precious*. While the word has the sense of "valuable" or "costly," it does not necessarily carry the meaning of "desirable." Perhaps it is a fault of a materialistic culture that we typically make the immediate correlation between cost and desirability. It is not as if God desires the death of a saint—this is clearly not the meaning of the verse. The idea is that because God treasures each of His "godly ones" (saints; in other words, believers in Christ), the death of each one is a big deal. He notices. He cares. They are costly to Him. One has only to think of Jesus with Jairus's daughter (Luke 8:49–56), with the widow of Nain (Luke 7:11–17), or at the tomb of Lazarus (John 11:33–44) to get the right idea about how the death of a saint is precious to God.

4. This is not a synonym for "pastor" of "professional church worker." It is not even limited to what occurs on Sunday morning during the time of worship. To live as God's servant does not even mean "doing things for Jesus." Living as God's servant means living in obedience to His will, doing what He has given you to do. That means that living as God's servant is primarily about living as the servant of your fellow creatures, because that is what God has given you to do. You live as God's servant by doing your vocation(s), serving others.

5. Recognition of the priceless value of each unique creature could be proven by an increased deference and humility before fellow creatures, especially before fellow believers. Another outstanding way of practicing godliness with fellow believers is to find greater ways to serve them—considering and then meeting their needs and desires—simply because they are of inestimable worth to their Creator and so, by extension, also to you.

Friday   Psalm 116:17-19

1. You probably did not put "standing up in church on Volunteer Sunday to a smattering of obligatory applause" at the top of this list. Nor was the "Christmas bonus" one of your treasured forms of being praised. Probably the most significant times of praise and appreciation were the ones that arose spontaneously, the ones that happened in private between you and one or two others, the words of thanks that you did not expect.

2. The implied response is the right one: "Of course not!" To humbly receive the thanks and appreciation of others and to thank God for the way that He used you to serve others fit together in wonderful symmetry. In fact, the godly reception of praise will usually defer that praise to God even as it graciously allows the recipient the opportunity to do the right thing by extending thanks and appreciation. The problems arise when pride injects itself into the occasion and leads to inflated self-importance, a sensitive ego, and a condescending attitude of entitlement to the praise of others.

3. The psalmist would have shed blood to offer his sacrifice, but Jesus' perfect sacrifice brought an end to the sacrifice of doves, goats, and bulls. For Christians, sacrificing is something altogether different. Paul put it powerfully and memorably: "Present your bodies as a living sacrifice, holy and acceptable to God" (Romans 12:1). By living life the way that God intended it to be lived, Christians offer exactly the right sort of sacrifice of thanksgiving.

4. Jerusalem, of course, is the site of the temple, and in the days of the Davidic monarchy, all worship in Israel was centered in, and restricted to, the Jerusalem temple. It was *the* holy place for the psalmist and all the people. While western Protestants have a tendency to treat all spaces and places with an irreverent sameness, there are holy places still today—places set aside and chosen by God where He gives His gifts. Ordinarily we call these places "church." They are holy because this is where God works through Word and Sacrament for the good of His people.

5. The psalmist wants to offer his praise of God where it can encourage others. Worship in isolation is never sufficient—faith in God and worship of God always take place in a corporate context, even if attended only by angels. Individuals, you

included, need to remember their responsibility to the wider Church and act accordingly. Praise of God can be quite infectious. When you have something to pray about or praise about, it is properly done where others will benefit and be infected by your prayer of thanks and joy.

GROUP BIBLE STUDY
(Questions are on pp. 92–93.)

1. *What was your most recent encounter with death? How should Christians think about death?*

It may have been a near miss in an automobile accident, a funeral visitation, or the untimely passing of your daughter's chameleon . . . death is never far from any of us. While Christians know that faith in Christ transforms death and removes its sting, they also know that death is not natural and is the frightening and frustrating wages of sin. Thus Christians do not treat death as being of no account, and they certainly do not embrace it as a happy release. Rather, they recognize that even Satan's apparent victory is not the final word, and even death gives way to resurrection life. Death is not a good thing, but neither is it the last thing.

2. *The opening line of the psalm is exceedingly terse and vibrant in Hebrew, literally, "I love for Yahweh listens." How does this opening set the tone of the entire psalm? What does it teach us about the vitality of our relationship with God and about the way that we pray?*

The first line—and, in truth, the entire psalm—breathes a sense of immediacy and spontaneity that is fresh and authentic. The psalmist appears almost breathless, as if he has only just come from the scene of his tight scrape with death. For the psalmist, faith is altogether real and relevant. His prayer life, represented by this psalm, radiates the joy and exuberance that were hallmarks of his relationship with Yahweh.

3. *What makes a prayer a* good *prayer? How does the prayer of verse 4 measure up?*

Other suggestions may be offered, but a great prayer is measured by two factors: is it offered in faith, and does it convey the need of the moment? Eloquence and literary form are merely ancillary and finally insignificant. By this standard, the single-line prayer of verse 4 is perfect simply as it is.

4. *Looking around at the world and the sorts of things that you and others experience, what conclusions would you reach about God's character? How would you respond to someone who argued that he saw no evidence to support the claim of verse 5?*

Life is not always a pleasant affair. Even apart from the manmade chaos and suffering that are imposed on us—and sometimes undeservedly so—there are so many "natural" disasters that, with what seems an arbitrary caprice, wreak devastation on men, women, and children. The forces of nature can amass a staggering body count with a sudden and brutal intensity that would shame the most ardent terrorist. Claims that God is gracious and compassionate may seem like absurd or delusional ravings to those who are struggling through times of agony. Such sufferers should not be "talked out" of their conviction that something has gone terribly wrong. Don't redefine evil. Rather, acknowledge the reality of evil, and then declare the greater reality of God's grace and compassion, proven in Christ and promised to those who hope in Him.

5. *How would you describe a "simple" person? Why would God preserve such people? What would you think about trying to live your life more simply? Simple* is a word that often conjures images of black buggies outrageously and incongruously tagged with orange SMV signs. The Amish describe themselves and their lives as "simple." It is usually a good thing to pursue simplicity and to streamline our lives, which tend to be cluttered with far too many things that demand attention—the more stuff you get, the more time, money, and thought it requires to take care of it. But the Hebrew word for *simple* is not a positive one. "The simple" had no merit or value; rather, they were gullible and unfocused, forever wandering into trouble. "The silly" is not too strong a translation. It is remarkable, then, that the psalmist readily identifies himself with this group of ridiculous no-accounts. Even more remarkable is the fact that God actually looks after them. It is not as if the "simple" garnered God's attention by their virtue. Quite the opposite; they earned His rebuke and rejection. But instead, they received His intervening grace. Such is the story of our own simple lives.

6. *Overwhelmed by the stunning reality of God's grace, the psalmist asks the only polite—the only* possible—*question (v. 12). What do you think of his answer (vv. 13–14)? What relevance does his answer have for Christians today?*

Readily recognizable from its use as an offertory in several settings of the Divine Service, in many ways, this three-verse section is one of the most remarkable passages in the entire Psalter. It can be argued that his answer captures exactly the dynamic reality that is the Christian life. "I will lift up the cup of salvation" is more insightfully (and legitimately) translated "I will lay claim as my own the cup of salvation." This sense fits wonderfully with what follows, and the message is clear and beautiful: The only thing to give God in response to His giving is to honor Him by receiving and cherishing the salvation that He gives. The way to thank God is to continue to call upon God. That takes care of the central and fundamental relationship of the Christian with the Creator. In verse 14, the psalmist picks up the other side of the Christian life: the responsibility to "pay my vows to the LORD." In other words, the believer needs to do what God wants to be done—he needs to live as the kind of creature that God intended. The Christian "pays his vows" not with animal sacrifices and not only with a check in the offering plate. He pays his vows by doing his vocations as God intended. He lives his life in service to others. This is the Christian life: Receive what God gives, do what He gives you to do.

7. *Twice (vv. 14 and 18), the psalmist asserts his commitment to pay his vows to the Lord and hopes that it may happen "in the presence of all His people." What does he have in mind? Why do you think this setting is so important to him? What should Christians learn from this today?*

The psalmist is eager to take his place in the public worship of Israel—in the temple. There he would present the appropriate sacrifices. There he would sing God's praises not only to God but to his fellow worshipers. There he would tell his story of deliverance. The psalmist needs the rest of the community of faith in order to fulfill his vows. He needs God's people if he is going to do what he needs to do. He can't wait to worship. The immediate lesson is that Christians need to gather for corporate worship because they, too, need to be part of the body of believers if they are to live faithfully the life God has given them to live. But the lesson is much more far-reaching than merely "Go to church!" The believer's dependence on the community extends far beyond Sunday morning's Divine Service. To do what God has given you to do, you need God's people. What you have been given to do is your vocation(s), and this you can do only in the midst of other people. You do your vocations not for God, but for others. Thus, *you* must "pay your vows," that is, do what God has given you to do, "in the presence of all God's people." It is the only place to do any vocation.

8. *While the death of every creature is significant to the Creator (Matthew 10:29), what is it that makes the death of God's saints actually precious (v. 15)? Think about the attitude conveyed by the Church's practices; how might they better communicate the idea that the death of a believer is precious?*

It is imperative to understand that verse 15 is not to be understood as if God approves, desires, or seeks the death of his followers. *Precious*, at least in this case, does not mean "sought after." As Jesus demonstrated throughout His ministry, death is a sad and anomalous intrusion into life that is of great importance to God. It is costly also to the Creator. Those who are trusting in Him, those who are His godly ones, are destined for participation in the eschatological fulfillment on the Last Day, of course, but death still intrudes, and God also grieves and finally transforms the sorrow and defeat of death into the laughter and victory of resurrection. The group can determine whether they believe the Church to be sufficiently reflecting a godly attitude toward death. A worthy part of the discussion, however, should be the extent to which cultural attitudes toward death have infiltrated the Church's understanding and practice. For example, contrary to cultural wisdom, death is not natural; it is not a mere gateway to a better existence; it is not a blessing or a cause for celebration.

9. *How is it true that verse 16 describes a move between two very different ways of being bound? What is binding you today?*

The psalm began with the writer "encompassed" by "the snares of death" (v. 3). He was trapped in the bonds of death. Now, on the other side of the ordeal, and coolly contemplating his newly redeemed life, the psalmist willingly submits to a new set of bonds: the bonds of slavery ("servant" is a bit too nice a translation) to the Lord (v. 16). That the writer repeats his chosen place before God, "I am Your servant, I am Your servant," indicates his resolve to live in the happy bondage of enslavement to his Creator, being fully committed to doing the things that matter to God. In many ways, the Christian life, lived as it is within the tension of being at once justified saint and broken sinner, is an ongoing battle over the bonds that will bind and control—whether those of God, or those of the world, or of Satan, or of the creeping, sometimes-terrifying fear of death.

10. *When all is said and done, why is "Praise the LORD!" a very good way to end a prayer?*

We have the well-established habit of concluding our prayers with an "Amen" usually preceded by some reference to Jesus' name. But an exuberant and expressive exclamation of "Hallelujah!" or "Praise the LORD!" is a favorite way for the psalmists to conclude their prayers and praises. Perhaps injecting a bit of novelty into the conclusion of prayers would highlight the freedom we have in our conversations with God and improve the caliber of our praying. It might be something to try in your own prayer life—a way to reignite some of the vibrancy and joy of prayer. In fact, it could be a great way to conclude your group's prayer.

DAILY STUDY QUESTIONS

Monday   Psalm 135:1–4

1. Like the author, you may have been sorely tried by experiences with sports or "volunteer" activities at church. Or perhaps being a husband or father has imposed demands and expectations you never dreamed of.

2. No reason is suggested. In fact, one of the great mysteries of salvation history is why God simply picked Abram and his descendants through Isaac and Jacob to be His chosen people. It is a mark of God's grace that He extends all of His blessings and benefits by His own choice without any merit or worthiness in the one He chooses.

3. The first is found in verse 3: "The LORD is good" and His name is "pleasant." In the following verse he argues that such praise is deserved because the Lord has chosen Jacob—the entire nation of Israel—for Himself. The first reason is founded on the very nature of God; simply by virtue of the fact that God is God and is therefore good and pleasant, He deserves the praise of His creatures. The second reason appeals to God's actions on behalf of His people. Not only is God intrinsically great and worthy of praise, but He has acted decisively on behalf of His people, choosing them for Himself. God is praised for who He is and for what He has done.

4. The words translated "Praise the LORD" are often left untranslated and have given us the English word *Hallelujah* (which is not English at all, of course, but Hebrew). In this case, the phrase has an imperative sense as it is used to encourage praise in particular from those who were at the temple. Thus the words are not idle wishes or simply expressions of delight. They are more like entreaties to fellow believers to live up to their callings.

5. Scripture tells us that God chose you before He laid the foundation of the world (Ephesians 1:3–6). But that choice was enacted when He called you to faith through the proclamation of the Word to you individually, whether at the font as an infant or by hearing the Word declared to you when you were older. This choice is always at the heart of our worship—had God not so chosen, you would not be able to worship, and because He *has* so chosen you, you have every reason in creation to sing His praise.

Tuesday   Psalm 135:5-7

1. While money and possessions frequently get top billing on the long list of competing gods, perhaps it is true that when all is said and done, the god most often given the position of sovereignty in our lives is simply the god of *self*.

2. The honest response might very well be "I have no idea—I just felt like it." This is typically the case when it comes to sin; we know what we should do, but for reasons that make no sense, we don't do it. Sometimes the desire to satisfy self *now* overwhelms the knowledge that we need to do something else that will ultimately bring us the most happiness and joy, but later. Sin is irrational.

3. There are a number of ways to answer this question, some better than others. We might appeal to what Scripture teaches us, or to what the Church has formed us to believe, or to what the philosophers have concluded about monotheism and the sovereignty of the Supreme Being, or even to what makes sense. Maybe the best answer, though, is the recognition of what God has done for you in creating you (the point made by these verses of the psalm), redeeming you, and preserving you. God's action in the Means of Grace, His love that drives this action, and the cross and tomb that make grace reality are the best proof of God's greatness.

4. It is clear that God is quite involved in every aspect of this world, directing even the smallest details of its operation—the mist in the morning, the lightning with the rain, the winds from His heavenly storage facilities. The idea of an absentee landlord who created and then stepped back to "let things take their course" is foreign to biblical faith.

5. The psalmist learned to see all the workings of creation as striking proof of God's majesty and concern for His people. The eyes of faith lead us to see all things in a way that honors God and His active role in every part of our lives. Seeing with such discernment can only eventuate in praise to such a God.

Wednesday   Psalm 135:8-12

1. While some of us have had the extra challenge of growing up without the benefit of a loving and caring father, we can all readily grant the important role a father plays in the life of a son—a role that combines many avenues of discipline, from tender words of encouragement to pointed rebuke tinged with righteous anger. Certainly, selective memory may be indicative of significant relational and emotional problems. But, perhaps more commonly, it may simply be the result of a compassionate memory that sees all things through the lens of honor and respect and recognizes the overriding context of love that directed even the occasional sharply

pointed corrective rebuke.

2. Any display of power that is out of our control and that has the potential to be unleashed on us should rightly terrify us! However, when the power that we witness is being wielded on our own behalf, that demonstration of might provides tremendous encouragement. It is a sign of love on our behalf. God's wrath should provoke both responses among His people. In the case of the exodus, Pharaoh's loss is Israel's gain.

3. Yes, this is one of those leading/misleading questions. In fact, God makes it very clear that He does *not* change—His character and His dealings with His creation are quite consistent, regardless of what initials accompany the date. BC or AD (or even BCE), God is still God. He still hates sin and promises to punish those who will not turn from their sin. Yes, He even continues to smite kings and rulers. And He still extends breathtaking grace to those who have been crushed by sin and its awful consequences and so desperately seek His mercy. There is not a "BC God" who is replaced by an "AD God."

4. The mention of actual nations and the names of specific kings forces us to acknowledge God's intervention in this world, not only in amorphous and indistinct ways, but in concrete and direct ways. God does things, and the biblical record will not let us forget this fact. This should also force us to move beyond thinking about God and His activity in vague generalities, and instead learn to recognize in our own lives His specific work in specific ways.

5. God has not promised you real estate. Your heritage is better. God has promised you a place in His eternal kingdom, a spot at His banquet table, a vocation in His perfectly restored new creation. This heritage is not only future tense; you taste it daily as you participate in the life of the Church, receiving the grace of Word and Sacrament, and as you delight in the wonders of God's good creation all around you—glimpses of the greater reality yet to appear.

Thursday   Psalm 135:13-18

1. You might recall the headstone of a family member, a prominent stone in a cemetery you frequently pass, or a remarkably beautiful or witty carving that is etched in your memory. Maybe you've already picked out your stone and its message, or maybe someone else will do it for you; regardless, the greater story of your stone will be told by those impacted by your life. This is the story that most deserves your attention.

2. Aside from the obvious connections that both are carved by artisans (at least

they used to be), carefully selected by men, meant to last, and typically carry spiritual overtones, the greater connection is the message about the individual associated with them that each delivers. While both are mute, a man's idols and a man's tombstone can say much about the man. It is also interesting to note that both are closely connected to death.

3. Of course, there are the standard idols of power, security, and financial prowess. But it is also important to recognize the idolatrous place sometimes given to things like career, leisure, and even family. An idol does not have to be universally recognized as a threat to true faith; the idols that consume people today are as unique and individualized as those who carve and worship them.

4. Different translations handle the wording here in different ways, but the straight translation has the Lord judging His people and having compassion on His servants. Typically, judging has a condemnatory connotation—though a judge at the county fair probably does far less condemning than commending. The point is that these two ideas are not in contradiction or even tension. The Old Testament often uses *judge* to mean "rule over" or "lead" (consider the content of the Book of Judges). And when God is judging or exercising authority over His people, He always does so according to His nature; that is, He shows compassion.

5. Not only are there eternal consequences for the worship of false gods—which are, in the last analysis, by far the most important consequences—but there are also immediate temporal consequences. Following false gods, allowing other things to take God's place and claim the center of your life and its priority, will cause you to become increasingly dull and unable to function as God designed you to function in relation to the rest of creation. Idolatry makes the idol worshiper more like a beast or a zombie than the living, acting, fully human being God intended when He created.

Friday   Psalm 135:19-21

1. Perhaps it was the conferral of an academic degree, an award for athletic accomplishment, a bonus at work, or the heartfelt congratulations of a friend. The point is to recognize that praise can come in many forms.

2. As is the case for the author of this devotion, our immediate thoughts may go to the arena of childhood sports, where the praise seemed rote and pointless. Or we might think of the way a carefully crafted "word of praise" can actually carry a strong negative message—damning with faint praise. Politicians and academics seem to be masters of this intricate art. Most parents can also recall the disconcerting experience of praising a child only to have the child react with despair because the compliment implied horrific things unimagined by the naive parent (for instance, praise for intel-

lectual accomplishments might seem like a curse to the child yearning for athletic success among his peers). Giving a good word of praise is not always easy.

3. While the word *bless* has taken on a more passive connotation in English usage—we "bless" those who sneeze and humbly hope for God's "blessing"—its use in the Psalms is little more than as a synonym for *praise*. To "bless God" is to acknowledge His sovereignty and His goodness in giving gifts. It is to extend honor and reverence. In short, it is to praise God.

4. The effect of the repeated exhortation "bless the Lord!" is a decided emphasis on the desired outcome. Like a drumbeat, and every bit as rhythmic as a pounding drum, the psalmist urges the listeners to do what is right: bless the Lord . . . bless the Lord . . . bless the Lord. The imperative is ultimately the indicative of faith. It is what creatures are created to do with no other gods before them, they worship the only true God. They bless Him.

5. Jerusalem was God's chosen city, the national capital, and the site of Israel's temple. *Zion* was the name of the specific hill on which the temple was built. To use these names is to remind the people of God's many ways of blessing them from the holy place that was Mount Zion. To think about God's faithful giving through His covenant presence with them in Jerusalem is to prompt loud praise. Because of fond memories or long-established habits, you should have your own "holy places" that move you to praise God by doing little more than thinking of them. It is God's intention that your congregation, the place where His Means of Grace are in action, would top this list of holy spots that engender praise.

GROUP BIBLE STUDY
(Questions are on pp. 118–119.)

1. Tell the group about a situation when you were genuinely afraid or in serious danger. How might it be possible for those kinds of memories to become a part of the praises you offer to God?

Even the bravest of men knows what it is to be afraid, and we all have faced dangerous circumstances. The very fact that you can now sit comfortably and discuss those events as memories is testimony to God's deliverance. The most horrifying experience is transformed into a reason to praise God simply because God is faithful and will always direct every outcome to His purpose.

2. The psalmist exhorts praise from the "servants of the LORD" who stand in the house and courts of God (vv. 1–2). Who might these people be? Why would they need to be encouraged to offer praise?

It is quite possible that the psalmist is thinking of the full-time servants who lived and worked at the temple: priests and Levites. It is also possible that he is encouraging all those who are gathered for worship to offer praise to God. Though one might be tempted to assume that such people would hardly need to be reminded to give God praise, "professional" servants as well as every other worshiper might benefit from such encouragement as a hedge against empty or routine worship or against "worship" that allows the focus to fall from God to self.

3. If we and the psalmist are strict monotheists (and we are), then what is meant in verse 5 by declaring Yahweh "above all gods"?

Monotheists believe that there is only one true God. This does not, however, eliminate the reality of idols that are acclaimed as gods who will actively compete with—and even displace—the true God. These idols may be the traditional "graven images," or they may be the more sophisticated forms of self-promotion that so often drive our lives. Of course, the reality of monotheism does not rule out the existence of powerful spiritual beings who also directly compete with God—sometimes the Bible's writers are willing to use the term *gods* to refer to these angelic or demonic beings. But of course, this is not meant to imply that such beings are in any way comparable to the one true God. Creatures are always in a class apart from God who alone is Creator and Lord.

4. *Verse 6 is quite striking in the simple and definitive declaration it makes: God does what He wants. How does this truth resonate with you? Does it encourage you? humble you? terrify you? What kind of problems does this bold truth raise?*

A God who does whatever He pleases can be quite disconcerting—especially if we live without faith and have no reason to assume a benevolent disposition from this God. We must admit that there are times in life when it seems as if the Creator and Lord of Life was a bit arbitrary in His dealings with us. Why does He bless some and apparently curse others? How do I assure a good standing before a capricious and omnipotent God? Even if faith overcomes these nagging questions, there remains the perennial problem of evil's continued existence and devastation—this in spite of our claim that whatever pleases God, He does. Naturally, the question is, why doesn't a loving, all-powerful God do something about the suffering and evil of this world? Scripture provides only one response, the lesson confessed by a repentant Job: God is Creator, and a creature has no business calling Him to justify Himself and His plan.

5. *Verses 6–14 are quite deliberate in their progression. What is the overall course of the "argument" in these verses? How does this parallel our own confessions of faith? What does this have to do with our praise of God?*

The sweep of the argument moves from the breadth and wonder of creation and God's continuing activity in the physical world (vv. 6–7) to His actions of redemption on behalf of His people (vv. 8–12), and it concludes with a look to God's faithful work for future generations and final judgment (vv. 13–14). This outline is precisely the outline of the Church's creeds from the First Article on creation through the Second Article on redemption and finishes with the promise of consummation at the Last Day. A God so powerful and so involved in our lives and welfare is a God who must be praised.

6. *Why was the giving of the land so significant to the people of Israel (v. 12)? What relevance does this have for Christians who praise God with this psalm?*

Giving the people a land meant stability and a future. They would have a place that was "theirs," a place where their progeny would be established and would thrive. Giving the land was giving Israel a status and an identity that would endure. While there are some Christians who insist on the continuing significance of the literal land of Israel (or Palestine or Canaan, depending on one's political proclivities) Scripture indicates that for the new Israel (Christ's Church—both Jews and Gentiles!), the Promised Land is all of creation at the final consummation when Christ restores everything according to the Father's creative intention. For Christians, Old Testament references to the land should immediately generate thoughts of our Lord's eternal eschatological kingdom, when every promise will be fulfilled.

7. If idols are merely and obviously the products of men, and men clearly know this, why do men continue to give them their attention and worship?

This question may generate some substantial discussion about the motives and needs of human beings. In the last analysis, however, the answer is simple: man can't help himself. Every man must have something at the center of his life to provide meaning, focus, and value to his life and its activities. That thing, as Luther argued in the Large Catechism, is properly that man's god—or, as the case may be, his idol. So even the most carnal, anti-spiritual man continues to build and worship idols, though he would strenuously deny the fact. Each man must have a god. Each man does have a god—even if that god is as pathetic and vain as his own self.

8. How does the repetitive structure of verses 16–17 work to strengthen the psalmist's point? What is the point that he makes in verse 18? Why is this true, and what warning does it have for people today?

The listing of each of the sense organs and then the corresponding absence of function highlights the futility of idolatry. These inventions of man's cunning are nothing more than dust collectors despite any resemblance they may bear to actual, God-created, functioning organs. They are insensible, unresponsive, impotent . . . dead. All idolaters inherit the traits of their chosen idol. They become emotionally, spiritually, and finally physically insensitive, unresponsive, impotent, and dead. This is so because men are created to be in relation to their Creator. Those who ignore this part of the natural law will always shrivel and degenerate into less than God intended, becoming *in*human—like the idols they worship. What you worship shapes what you are and what you become.

9. What is being conveyed by the three separate exhortations to the "houses" of Israel, Aaron, and Levi in verses 19–20? What might this threefold exhortation say to those today who wrestle with the relationship between the laity and the clergy?

Each house represents the heirs of a unique and specific portion of the worshiping community. "Israel" refers to all the people—the entire community of faith with a particular emphasis on the laity. Aaron's descendants are the priests, what we would today consider clergy. The Levites are neither priests nor laity, but in the special serving group of individuals who assisted the priests in the operation of the temple, the sacrifices, and the worship of the nation. The exhortation is directed to all those who worship, laity and clergy alike. Perhaps it is not reading too much into the text to see here a recognition of the distinction between the unique roles of each group (priests are not laity or Levites—and vice versa, twice), yet each group carries the same responsibility of offering praise to God. One group cannot assume the work to be the task of another group. We all must give ourselves fully to blessing

God, but this does not mean that we all do the same sorts of things. Each does what he has been given to do.

10. *What is the best way to praise (or bless) God? Is it possible to praise Him if the worship is habitual or rote? Do actions praise God better than songs?*

The author of this week's devotions is quite right. Praising God is a whole-life thing and not limited to an hour on Sunday morning or singing along with a recording or humming a "praise" tune in your head. Doing what God created you to do is, in fact, the highest form of praise. This is how the stars, trees, and rocks praise God—though they are limited in their "praise capabilities" by lack of tongues and lungs. Simply by doing what God created them to do, they praise God. When you offer God worship—as you should, regardless of how you "feel in your heart" about it, it is the right thing to do and *is* praise. Thus, even rote worship that is done out of habit can accomplish its purpose of directing the worshiper back to the realities that matter—re-grounding the person in the truth of God's sovereignty and glory. Praise is actually more for the good of the creature who must offer praise to be a "right" creature than it is for God who exists whole and complete with or without a creature's praise, heartfelt or otherwise. In other words, God does not need our praise, but for our own sakes, we need to praise Him. Singing is great praise, but so is mowing the lawn or spending an evening talking with your wife or playing with your kids. All of life is praise to God when it is lived as God intended it to be lived—which, of course, includes the commitment to regular (at least weekly) corporate worship.

DAILY STUDY QUESTIONS

Monday   Psalm 145:1-3

1. You may recall a distant childhood memory; or it may be a recent interaction between you and your wife, when you were extended grace that you neither deserved nor expected. God provides us with many such occasions—reminders of the fundamental reality of His way of grace with us.

2. Memories of old gifts have their place in the list of proof of God's love, but it is the recent and personal giving that is perhaps most potent. To a list including the birth of Christ as evidence of God's love for humanity, you can add the day of your Baptism as proof of God's love for you individually, as through the grace of those sacramental waters, He called you to be His very own. You can also remember the time—hopefully only a few days ago—when your Lord communed with you through bread and wine and gave you the assurance of complete forgiveness and an identity that lasts for eternity.

3. It seems quite fitting in the context of faith to see in David's words more than a bit of hyperbole. For those of us who live by faith in Christ, David's confident promise is an assertion of our hope in the resurrection and the reality that we will indeed offer our praise to God forever and ever—nothing, not even death, will stop that stream of praise.

4. "One generation shall commend Your works to another." David is confident that this is the way that God's community of faith will function. In today's devotion, we witness precisely this taking place: one generation lives the grace of God, giving an Etch A Sketch® that is undeserved, and the generation receiving the grace continues to tell the story until the next generation, today's author, can tell the story in detail. The generations continue to tell the story of God's grace individually extended in an Etch A Sketch® and universally delivered in a Bethlehem stable.

5. The personal blessings of God's grace that we experience in our routine interactions with one another are some of the most important works that need to be shared and celebrated with the next generation. These become part of the powerful narrative that defines each individual life, and they provide powerful clues about identity and life purpose. Of course, the grand works that God has done on behalf of the whole of creation—His works of redemption history—also need to be declared and rehearsed again and again.

Tuesday   Psalm 145:4-9

1. At the top of the list, even ahead of shelter, food, and clothing, is a sense of identity and purpose; without these, all the material goods in the world will not be able to create a safe harbor for life. As you think about your own life, consider how critical it is for that sense of purposeful identity to be firmly in place in your own self-understanding, and how vital it is for you to have the sense that you are dwelling in a safe harbor despite the storms that may be surging around you.

2. One of the great blessings of faith is the identity that God provides as He makes clear that you are His very own and that you live to accomplish His purposes: using your gifts, skills, and time to serve those around you. Such an unwavering and consistent sense of self and purpose is a gift that many Christians take for granted, but it is one of inestimable value.

3. The idea of meditation definitely carries some negative freight for most of us—we think a Hindu holy man on top of a snow-covered peak, frozen in the lotus position with a look of serenity etched on his countenance. But David opens the world of meditation much wider: meditate on God's wonderful works. In other words, spend some time thinking about something that God has done. The exciting thing about this suggestion is that virtually anything in creation is a result of God's work, and so is a worthy object of meditation—provided that the meditation is practiced within the context of faith that celebrates God as the source and sustainer of that creation that is occupying your thoughts. In other words, thinking long and hard about some wonder of creation or some philosophical principle built into the world can be as worshipful as singing a "praise song"; it may, in fact, be *more* worshipful as it leads you to marvel at God's greatness. So let you mind dwell on some facet of God's wonderful works. There—you've just meditated!

4. Clearly, we do worship an awesome and a great God, but *awesome* and *great* are rather general words and traits that can also be applied to powers and authority that is not necessarily benevolent. Hence, the repeated Old Testament reminder of God's grace, mercy, loving kindness, and slowness to anger are a welcome addition to the character and being of our God who is so worthy of praise. God's greatness and awesome power are directed toward compassion, pity, and mercy.

5. While some might try to suggest certain settings or occasions when God's glorious acts, goodness, and righteousness should not be declared, David seems to imply that the man of faith will be so overwhelmed and so enthralled with God's character and might exercised on his behalf that silence about this God is impossible—words about God and His glory keep slipping out and are never far from the

lips of His people. Of course, wisdom calls for discretion and good timing so that the words of praise to God ring with joy and truth and serve to honor God in whatever setting they may be spoken. The challenge to us is to live in such a way and with such awareness of God that we are always ready for and eagerly seeking opportunities to declare what we know of our God.

Wednesday   Psalm 145:10–13

1. It is likely relatively easy to list the negatives: being subject to arbitrary laws, taxation without representation, no recourse when injustice comes from the king or queen. But citizens of democracies also recognize the shortcomings of such majority rule and can yearn for the security, consistency, and efficiency of a monarchy. In fact, it can be argued that every criticism of monarchy is blunted if the monarch is truly benevolent and ruling for the good of his subjects. God's kingdom, then, *is* the ideal we all eagerly anticipate.

2. Some Christians can give an exact date—the day that Baptism brought them into God's kingdom. Others can remember the precise moment when they finally turned in repentance and received what God had for so long been so eager to give. Others may not remember the day or time or circumstances; they simply know that they believe and that God is their Lord. The entry process matters little, really. Subjects are subjects. Of course, actually living purposefully as God's subject is assumed of all who claim to be part of God's kingdom.

3. Those who have been citizens of the true kingdom for their whole lives have the benefit of a life that has always been lived in the light of God's grace and truth— an enormous blessing indeed. Converts later in life, however, have the advantage of being able to recognize the profound contrast between life outside the Kingdom and life as a subject of the King. A sense of exuberant relief and joy are, perhaps, more typical of these citizens—they have firsthand experience of what they have gained as members of God's kingdom.

4. At times it may seem that those with worldly power and prestige are not to be troubled with the trivial problems of individual citizens. They may seem to be shielded from the unseemly things of life, kept away from the lowly and the down-trodden—even though, in all likelihood, they had a hand in driving the lowly and downtrodden to their sorry plight. But God is no ordinary king. He is a King who sustains and raises *all* who fall and *all* who are downtrodden—not just one lucky loser who receives the choreographed ministrations of a head of state as a symbolic gesture of compassion for the cameras. God is not interested in photo ops. He is committed to His people and their eternal well-being. Such a King has never been known in this broken world. Such a King is our profound hope.

5. The image of creatures waiting and looking for divine sustenance is captured well by farm animals awaiting their daily feeding or the family pet waiting at the cupboard and looking with anticipation at his master. Creatures know the source of their provisions. Humans, of course, have a tendency to forget to look to God and often wrongly assume that other, secondary providers are more relevant. But whether they are cognizant of the fact or not, all creatures—including all human beings—are fully dependent on God and His gracious provision. It is the wise creature who learns to keep his eyes on the true Giver and to acknowledge Him with appropriate praise.

Thursday   Psalm 145:14–17

1. Sadly, this broken world overflows with "shocking" stories of the fall of saints. The Bible brims with vivid and sometimes sordid accounts, and our own life experiences are peppered with more of these stories than we care to remember or admit. The hard but reluctantly conceded lesson is altogether disconcerting: none is immune. As the adage so accurately if painfully asserts, "There, but for the grace of God, go I."

2. The truth of every man's fallibility is difficult to acknowledge simply for the fact of human pride. None of us is eager to confess his own incapacity and failing. Pride and the sense of self-preservation drive us to deny the truth and to perpetuate the lies of self-righteousness and worth. But, difficult as it is, this is a lesson that must be learned, or faith will not grow. The prerequisite to faith is a broken heart. We must fall and fall utterly, with no hope of reclamation, before God's forgiveness and gift of faith will have any meaning or value. Actually, it is not critical that you realize that *everyone* falls; it is sufficient that you come to terms with the hard fact that *you* fall . . . and fall completely.

3. God's nearness is not to be understood spatially (as in, "God's sitting in the chair next to mine"), but relationally. We would be more likely to say, "God is close to those who call upon Him." Of course, closeness is about emotional and relational connections. You can be close to someone who is halfway around the world. It is exactly right that God is close to those who pray to Him. Prayer is indicative of a relationship of trust. When your eyes look to God and you call upon Him, He is near, He is close to you. Of course, if a man is living outside God's will, he certainly is not close to God, and vice versa. In that case, God's nearness is quite an intimidating and disquieting thought.

4. God promises to be close to "all who call on Him"—those who turn to Him in humble trust. And God promises to "[fulfill] the desire of those who fear Him."

Finally, God assures those who cry to Him that He will "[save] them." It seems that many in our culture assume that it is simply God's job to answer prayer and make life good for those who ask nicely. David makes clear, however, that these tremendous promises are extended only to those who call on Him and fear Him. In other words, the promises to be near and to fulfill desires are given only to those who live before God in a relationship of trust and faith. Christians should find tremendous comfort in these promises, but those without faith have no basis for claiming these promises for themselves.

5. Nowadays, the word *keep* is not widely used in the sense of "protect and safeguard"; it typically means little more than "retain," as in "keep your ticket stub." But when God keeps you, He does more than merely not throw you back. God actively works to protect you . . . and more than that, He orchestrates His plan to fulfill your desires, to complete you. All of God's powerful grace is at work for your eternal well-being. Such knowledge should give you great confidence and undying hope as you face whatever the new day brings.

Friday   Psalm 145:18–21

1. Most of us operate with many mistaken assumptions about what it means to praise God. While it may seem a bit hard to believe, at least according to your usual understandings, cries of distress and groans of suffering are praise when these sounds are directed to God as the only source of hope and the only means of relief.

2. It is freeing to recognize that cries for rescue and shouts of misery are not harsh sounds in the ears of our God, but are the sounds of praise. God hears these pleas as signs of our dependence on Him and our confession of our creaturely nature that waits for God's deliverance. Such a rich concept of praise allows tremendous honesty and realism to fill our prayers and our relationship with God. We are not required to play games with God, singing some sentimental praise song on the outside when our hearts are breaking on the inside. Better praise by far is a desperate appeal for God's mercy.

3. God made us material as well as spiritual creatures, so it is quite fitting that we praise God not only with our minds and "souls" but also with our physical selves. There is the additional benefit that words prayed aloud are actually heard and so reinforced. Somehow, from our human perspective, putting thoughts into actual spoken words makes them more real and substantial.

4. The effect is to reaffirm that David's view is not narrow or constrained only to his "personal relationship" with God. David recognizes that he is only one small part of all flesh and that the praise of creation is universal in scope. The whole creation,

including David and his mouth, offers praise to God. We live always as members of a wider community—in this case, the widest possible community of all creation. In a culture so enamored of rabid individualism as ours is, such reminders can hardly be overemphasized.

5. God's kingdom will be a material, physical kingdom that will include all *flesh*. This point is made all the more compelling by the fact of the incarnation. Christ, with human flesh, will rule over creation in its full, glorious, God-given materiality. We anticipate the resurrection and the restoration of creation, not some immaterial "spirit world" eternity.

GROUP BIBLE STUDY
(Questions are on pp. 148–149.)

1. *What are some of the specific, tangible things that God has done for you in the last week that rightly should move you to praise Him?*

Sometimes a few moments of reflection are necessary to enable each partici-pant in the study to be able to identify proofs of God's grace and mercy. In fact, it may well be the case that an individual or even an entire group may be undergoing a time of severe trial that makes a declaration of divine mercy seem almost absurd. It is precisely at this moment that it is most necessary to readjust our human perspective and so learn to acknowledge the liberal abundance of God's gracious giving to us. If the list is slow to materialize, try starting with life itself, Baptism, the forgiveness of sins, and the Church—all of which are present realities for every man.

2. *In the first verse, David declares his praise to God and then names Him "King." What does this title convey about God and about our relationship with Him?*

It is possible that the word or name *God* can become a bit of an abstraction with people supplying many erroneous ideas about what God would or would not do or allowing God to slip into some sort of ethereal realm disconnected from real life. Naming God as King makes Him immediately relevant. Even if we don't live in a monarchy ourselves, we understand about kings and their authority and majesty. We know how to treat kings. More importantly, we recognize that kings are part of real life and that what they do can have significant impact on their subjects' lives. Finally, kings aren't concepts or forces; they are real men with real personalities with whom it is possible to have a vital and dynamic relationship. You can talk to a king, you can appeal to a king, you can give honor to a king. You can't do any of those things to an idea or a principle.

3. *What does verse 4 teach us about the content of our praise? How might this sort of prais-ing of God differ from a typical understanding of what it means to praise God?*

"Praising God" has become associated with gatherings of serene worshipers who are singing and praying in near ecstasy as they are moved by the words of a song that fills the place with its infectious sound; often they are moved to physical motion as they gently sway with the rhythm of the "praise." Praising God is something done in church—or at least around a campfire. Praising God is something highly emo-tional. Praising God is like cheering for God the way one cheers for a great athlete or performer. Such are the assumed ideas about what praise must be. While the psalmist doesn't necessarily negate or disdain these ideas, he certainly is not content to allow such thoughts to suffice as a complete definition of praise. Rightly, he teaches that praise is tied to the specific and concrete actions of God in His dealings with His people. To put it simply, telling stories to one another about God's great deeds *is* profound praise of God. A father reading a Bible story to his daughter is praising God. Teaching a son a lesson about God's way of handling a typical teenage challenge is praising God. Declaring God's mighty acts in creation and in the preservation of creation takes on many forms—hence, praising God takes on many forms. Following David's words, we can see that while a great hymn celebrating God's creation or Christ's resurrection is praising God, so also is the sermon or the reception of the Lord's Supper.

4. *How does verse 8 provide not only a stirring motivation to praise, but also profound insight into the true greatness and glory of God? What evidence of this definition of God's character have you witnessed lately?*

Verse 8 is actually a quotation of a much older text: Exodus 34:6, the encounter between Moses and the Lord on Mount Sinai when God fulfilled Moses' desire to see God's glory. By offering these words as His "glory passed before [Moses]," God was in effect declaring that His glory is to show grace and mercy. Mercy *is* God's glory. Obviously, this helps to put the glory of the cross in the proper light. It is the very giving of Himself for us—what looks to us like abject humiliation and degradation—that is God's glory and the cause of our praise. God's mercy and grace extend to us all, daily, in many ways, including, of course, through Word and Sacrament.

5. *Why might this psalm put such a strong emphasis on the idea of God as king and we as subjects of His kingdom? How can this psalm's (actually, the whole Bible's) emphasis on monarchic images be made relevant to people infatuated with the leveling equality of democracy?*

David knew well what it meant to be a king responsible for the welfare of his people. And he knew that only God was able to do this task the way it needed to be done—with complete compassion and without any selfish motive. Only God can wield absolute power with absolute goodness. Citizens of western democracies have been thoroughly indoctrinated in a love for the democratic ideal; this is true. But as citizens of these democracies, they are also quite familiar and often equally frustrated with the shortcomings of this form of government. Perhaps the image of the truly benevolent King is not such a difficult concept. The natural law itself teaches us to yearn for the kind of grace-driven hierarchy that will be established in our Lord's eternal kingdom. The petty and evil monarchs and dictators of this world have nothing in common with God's rule.

6. Many will recognize verses 15–16 as a table prayer, one that was suggested and encouraged by Luther. What is the significance of God having an open hand? How should this image encourage His people to pray?

It is significant that in artwork, the *manus dei* (the "hand of God") is always depicted as open and extended toward His creation in blessing. God does not shake His fist or clench His fingers into a tight ball, refusing to release His gifts. His hand is ever open, ever delivering the blessings of His grace. Such a posture assures us that God is disposed to look on us favorably and that He yearns to hear and answer our prayers.

7. David makes some rather bold and extensive assertions about what God will do for His people (vv. 18–20). He is near. He fulfills desires. He saves. He keeps. Given the extent of these promises, what kind of life should Christians expect to live? What shadow appears in these verses—a hint of what David expects from life?

Taken together, it would seem that Christians have it made and should fully expect to live a charmed life free from pain, suffering, and difficulties—aside from the mild and short-lived forms of these challenges that God might use on occasion in order to make life even better. Many Christians insist on precisely this view of life and assume that anyone experiencing anything other than a blessing parade must be doing something wrong and living outside God's good graces. Anyone who knows David and his psalms knows better, of course. David exemplifies the man who does what is right (well, most of the time) and who lives before God in humble faith. Nevertheless, David's life is a story of unrelenting hardship, heartache, and suffering (running from Saul, falling into devastating personal sin, watching his family struggle and fail). David knew that "the wicked" were still around and that they still had the ability to rain misery and torture on anyone's parade, believer or not. Christians do not get a free pass from life's struggles. There is no guarantee that the days of this life will be ceaseless happiness and pleasure for the Christian; in fact, Scripture is clear that Christians should expect the opposite. So we wait for the fulfillment of God's glorious promises; we wait for Christ's appearing, when all will be fulfilled.

8. Is the second part of verse 20 somehow out of place in this psalm, or is it a necessary aspect of the reasons that creatures have to praise God? What is the basis for your answer?

With David, we praise God for His righteousness and His justice; these are essential to the character of God, who is the object of our praise. God's justice demands the punishment of the wicked, so David is not introducing an odd negative counterpoint to an otherwise perfectly positive psalm of praise. The destruction of the wicked is a reason to praise God.

9. *This is the last psalm of David to appear in the Psalter. What about this psalm makes it a fitting conclusion to David's collection of songs, petitions, and praises? How does the psalm have a personal yet more universal and inclusive appeal? What does this teach us about the ways that we praise God?*

While it is impossible to tell by reading the psalm in English, this is an acrostic psalm. Each verse in the Hebrew text begins with a successive letter of the Hebrew alphabet. Essentially, then, David is offering his praises to God, covering "everything from *A* to *Z*." Many of David's psalms are quite personal in nature, describing his own dealings with life and God. This psalm, however, has a more outward look, as it consistently makes reference to "men" in general and to "all who love Him" and even to "all flesh." All of creation is involved in praising God. While we certainly offer individual praises to God, our praise is only one part of the corporate praise of the whole creation. So we learn to "harmonize," not only with fellow believers (during the Divine Service, for sure), but with all fellow creatures as we joyfully do the things given us to do by our Creator. Praise is a very material, earthbound action, not some sort of ecstatic "spiritual" experience.

10. *What concrete and specific changes can you make in your own prayer life to better reflect what you have learned about praise through your study of this psalm?*

Each participant should be able to offer some thoughts about ways in which his prayer life might be enhanced or altered by David's teaching. This might include in particular a greater appreciation of the latitude of praise, which includes also our cries for help and groans of misery. Another aspect of this psalm that deserves greater emphasis in our prayers is the connectedness that we all have with the rest of creation. Participants can offer suggestions on ways that their praying can better reflect these great truths.

DAILY STUDY QUESTIONS

Monday   Psalm 148:1–3

1. Some things are, by their very nature, extraordinary and wonderful: a waterfall, a mountain, the view from the top of the mountain. Any of these things has the capacity to provoke praise by the sheer fact of its existence. When you scale a peak, scan the far horizon, and breathe out "Awesome!" you have experienced what amounts to involuntary praise. It can't be helped. The thing must have the praise.

2. This is the essence of holiness. God is God. For no other reason than that He is God, He is worthy of profound praise—like experiencing a waterfall and, without thinking, shouting "Wow!" Of course, God's very being is infinitely more praise-worthy than anything in creation, but the idea holds: God doesn't have to *do* anything to be worthy of praise. His being demands it.

3. Though they may not have the blessing (or is it a burden?) of being able to speak or sing, the mute members of creation absolutely *do* offer praise to God. They praise their Creator by the very fact of their existence and by their unwavering obedience to His set plan for them.

4. The typical assumption is that first one is blessed and then the praise follows. But the author of this devotion challenges this notion—as does Scripture! Often blessings are realized—that is, life tends to work better—after the right relationship with God has been established. This right relationship with God definitely includes praise for the sake of His holiness . . . quite apart from what good things have or have not been experienced. Praising rightly has remarkable power to align all the other parts of life.

5. It is entirely possible, even as mature Christian people, that without realizing it, we allow long periods of time to elapse without intentionally and directly offering praise to God.

Tuesday   Psalm 148:4–6

1. When it comes to questions about the origins of the universe, it is not unusual for Christians to progress (evolve!?) through a process like the one mentioned in the devotion. Perhaps you are still at one of the points at which you struggle with the idea of God actually creating in the way that Genesis 1–3 describes it. While the place of science within the narrative of salvation and faith lies well outside the parameters of this study, it is worth noting that maturity in faith is typically accom-

panied by a willingness to grant God latitude to do whatever He wants, however He wants—including creating the universe in six twenty-four–hour days.

2. Confessing that God is the source and the sustainer of all things and that God has established the "laws of nature" that direct the whole of creation will cultivate an attitude of profound interest in the creation and respect for what God has willed for His creation. A foundation of faith also encourages humility and a willingness to admit the limits and ignorance inherent in creatureliness.

3. Creation is not a labor-intensive process for God, nor something that demands a series of hearings or consultations with the members of creation. God speaks and things come into existence . . . period. There is no better demonstration of God's absolute authority. All things depend on God, and God does not depend on or need anything within the creation. This verse makes it clear: God is not a *part* of the creation. He is Lord over the creation.

4. While the text does not spell out the exact content of this enduring decree, the context of creation and the orderliness of that creation implicit in these verses point to a related decree. While God has made many lasting decrees, this one should be understood as the decree of the directing design, or the natural law, that guides the functioning and interactions of the creation.

5. Christians certainly have reason to be confident as they step out into God's creation—enormous and powerful as it is, it is still subject to God's rule, and therefore it is not to be feared or revered. Rather, man, according to the same guiding law that God has established, or "built in," to the creation, finds his right place in relationship with the creation and does what God put him on this earth to do: he cares for the creation and delights in God's good gifts delivered in the creation.

Wednesday Psalm 148:7–12

1. God's providence is a continuing reality, ever at work guiding and directing the course of this world for the good of His people and for the fulfillment of His plan. Because God's typical modus operandi is altogether subtle and cooperative with "natural forces," we tend to overlook or dismiss the fact of God's activity in and through all these things. A heightened awareness of God's work makes providence a present source of comfort and hope.

2. It is a fundamental component of our human makeup. We like to be wowed. Perhaps the big and showy interventions of God's power make us more certain of His presence and concern, or maybe we like the feeling of being so special that we deserve such attention. Maybe we just like to show off, and we appreciate it when

God does a little grandstanding. The unfortunate result is that we miss the wonder of God's steady and wise provision for His people through the routine and mundane things of life.

3. Starting in the ocean's depths, the psalmist moves next to the sky and its powerful "citizens" ("fire and hail, snow and mist, stormy wind") before reaching land, where he calls on the land itself and its flora before finally extending the invitation to praise even to the human members of the creation. The fact that all of these disparate components of the creation are subject to God's authority—evidenced by their obligation to praise Him—reassures us that nothing lies outside God's providential control.

4. Exactly what the psalmist had in mind with "great sea creatures" is hard to know. But by beginning his tour of earth in the seas, it is reasonable that he would include the most wonderful and captivating creatures that were known to dwell there. Of course, an ancient dweller in the Judean hill country cannot be expected to be overly familiar with marine life, so "great sea creatures" essentially covers all possibilities. It is also worth remembering that the sea was associated with chaos and evil, and it was considered the dwelling place of that which was opposed to God. That even the creatures of the deep are enlisted in the praise of God indicates the absolute sovereignty of the Lord.

5. By calling kings, princes, and judges to participate in the Psalm 148 praise-fest, the psalmist is making it clear that not even the cultural elites are exempt from the responsibility to praise the Creator. In our day when "beautiful people," great athletes, and celebrities garner privileges and "perks" beyond the imagination of the ordinary masses of people, and when the opinions of "experts" are accorded the status of reverence and awe, it is good to remember that men are just men. All are equally fallible, all are equally responsible for keeping the commandment and offering praise, and all are equal before the Creator.

Thursday   Psalm 148:13

1. The devotion's author is correct: true praise of God always produces a sense of contentment because in praising God and His greatness, you gain the assurance of God's grace and mercy at work in your own life. To praise God is to celebrate His mercy and power that work for your good. Praise like that cultivates a sense of contentment. Praise is the foundational action because apart from a faith relationship with the Creator, true contentment is impossible.

2. Some psychologists will use their "hierarchy of needs" and offer a confident, scientific response to the question that takes into account material, physical,

emotional, relational, and spiritual needs among others. The Christian can offer a simpler answer: "As much as God decides to give me." The lesson is not painlessly learned, of course. But the believer strives to grow in his Christian maturity so that he can also say, "I have learned to be content in any circumstance."

3. Like any other virtue, contentment absolutely can be learned. Surprisingly, the best course to follow to learn contentment is the deliberate and consistent practice of praising God. When one recognizes God's glory and acknowledges God's place as Lord and Master of all that is, he realizes that what he has is what God has determined is best for him to have. In a heart well cultivated by the adoration of God and trust in His good plan, discontentment cannot grow.

4. God *is* His name. There is no distinction between His name and His being. There is no other being in the category named "God" besides the only God there is. God is God. His name is His being. Thus, to praise God's name is no different from praising God.

5. Magnificent as the most spectacular members of creation in heaven and on earth may be, God is infinitely greater. Given that the first twelve verses methodically recount some of those great creations and call them to praise the Creator, the declaration at the end of verse 13 is all the more dramatic: consider all those wonderful things on earth and in heaven . . . God is far above them all. A God so great *must* be praised. Start now, and find a way to do it all day.

Friday   Psalm 148:14

1. Nothing . . . the answer must be nothing; you have done nothing to prompt God to love you, because all that you have done is shot through with sin and thus repulsive to God.

2. We are never the ones who make the first move. We are not even "godly ones" until God by grace makes us that way. This is the point of justification by grace through faith alone—God does it all; we simply receive what He delivers.

3. God's work of doing the Gospel to His people is always intimate and personal. He saves you. The gift of Baptism delivers to you what Christ, *the* horn of God's salvation, accomplished for you in His death and resurrection. God continues to be present in your life, and His gifts of Word and Sacrament are the means by which He keeps lifting up the horn of salvation for you. There may be singular instances of God's intervention for you in dramatic and miraculous ways, but even better are the ordinary yet miraculous ways that God works in your life. The last time you attended Divine Service, your most recent reception of the Lord's Supper, the last absolution

spoken to you—these are the ways that God lifts the horn for you.

4. The fact that the Second Person of the Trinity, the Son, became a true human being is the ultimate nearness of God to man. God has taken what it is to be human and has literally joined that perfect humanity to the divine nature. There is no closer bond possible. That in Christ, God took human flesh and blood into Himself means the most intimate closeness possible in your relationship with God. No metamorphosis is necessary. God loves humans as humans. The human that God created you to be is united with God in the reality of the incarnation and so, in Christ, you, too, are near to God.

5. After rehearsing all the wonders of the creation and calling each successive member of that universal community to praise the Creator, the psalmist arrives at the most incredible wonder of all: the Gospel. That this awesome God would work to save His people and would dwell near them is the supreme motivation to praise. In light of all that the psalm has considered, the creature is overwhelmed and breathless, and so "Praise the Lord!" whether shouted, whispered, chanted, or repeated a hundred times in sheer amazement and delight, is the only fitting response and conclusion.

GROUP BIBLE STUDY
(Questions are on pp. 174–175.)

1. *What are some of the largest worship gatherings in which you have participated? Which one was most meaningful to you? What was it like?*

Sometimes bigger is not better. Still, there is something remarkable about being part of an enormous gathering of believers all offering praise to God. Of course, this is the idea that is driving this psalm.

2. *What plan or order seems to be directing the writer as he works his way through the list of creatures invited to join in the praise of God? What message does this structure convey to the reader?*

This is no random list of members of the creation that happen to come to mind. The psalmist starts high and wide in the heavens and then moves into the earth's atmosphere where the flow is from the depths up to the heights before finally extending the invitation to praise to people. The enormous, encompassing sweep of the psalm reinforces the place of God within the universe—He is Lord and Master of *all*.

3. *One of the early Soviet cosmonauts infamously attacked belief in God by quipping from orbit that although he was traveling in the heavens, he had seen no sign of God. How might the psalmist respond to such a comment? How does a person's worldview affect what he sees?*

The cosmonaut found what he sought—nothing. Convinced of God's reality, holiness, and grace, the psalmist, on the other hand, would see only breathtaking evidence of God's presence. What a person believes and confesses dramatically dictates what he is able to see in the world around him.

4. *As the psalmist compiles his invitation list, he includes many members of creation that "naturally" praise God (sun and moon, hills and trees) and others that praise Him by vocation (angels and heavenly hosts). Why does he exhort creatures to praise when they already do it without being told?*

The exhortation is extended to all extremes of creation—invisible as well as visible. The psalmist is not encouraging angels, hosts, and inanimate nature to correct a deficiency in the caliber of their praise or to change something that is currently inadequate. The call for their praise serves the interest of both writer and reader by pointing to the breadth and depth of God's creation. We are reminded that creation includes far more than human beings—precious as we may be. All of creation is involved in the praise of God, and we men should recognize our place within this grand plan. Another way of thinking about this exhortation to do what is already being done is to realize that the encouragement to do something need not imply that it is not currently already being done. Think of the standard encouragements that pepper our farewells: "Drive carefully," "Study hard," "Be good," and so on. It is not as if these are new thoughts, or behaviors that are still in the offing. We say these things because in our zeal and love, we want to encourage even more of the good behavior. The psalmist operates with a similar agenda.

5. *In verses 5 and 6, the psalmist makes a strong point about the origin of the many invisible and heavenly beings he has mentioned. Why does he need to stress that they were created by God with little more effort or energy than the speaking of a word? What sort of errors in the theology and thinking of twenty-first–century Christians might be prevented by a better grasp of this reality?*

In the ancient world, and still in a sense in the modern world, worship of the great members of creation was a continual temptation. The psalmist gives the orthodox reaction to such idolatry: all things exist only by the command of God. Creatures are, therefore, never worthy of worship. Only the Creator deserves such praise. A reminder that even the greatest wonders of creation are still only the result of God's work would help to keep our worldview grounded in God's truth rather than in "nature's law" or the insights of science or philosophy. There is nothing more fundamental or foundational than God and His active will. *Everything* else is derived and should be considered accordingly.

6. *What does it mean that the "stormy wind" also fulfills God's Word? What word does it fulfill? How do we explain to people (to ourselves!?) that "natural disasters" caused by the stormy wind are actually fulfilling God's Word?*

The word being fulfilled is not disclosed, but the context would indicate that it is God's providential word—the plan that He has for the right functioning of His creation. The problem of natural disasters caused by natural forces that are clearly under the control of the Creator is not easily solved, of course. In fact, this side of Christ's Second Coming, there is no adequate solution beyond claiming the promises of God and trusting the providence of God—even when, from our perspective, there is precious little evidence of such caring providence. The hard truth is that God does use even the worst disasters within His plan, but at the same time does not wish or relish the evil that is done. Unsatisfactory as this is to our sense of logic and justice, faith must yield to revelation and cling to God's promise to bring all things to their right end. The cross and empty tomb provide good cause for such robust faith, even in the face of horrific disasters.

7. How different are the groups of people listed in verses 11 and 12? What is the one thing that has the potential to unite and bind them? What implications does this hold for interactions between different cultures and between competing nation states?

By intention, the psalmist describes widely variant groups of people, from the elite to the common, from the young to the very old. What all of them have in common is their creatureliness. All of them owe God their praise. Unity comes as they do what it is their duty to do: they praise God and find in that action true unity. Ultimately, despite the best attempts at "understanding and tolerance," the only things that truly unite different people are their common bond to their Creator and their common need to offer Him their praise. True world peace only occurs when every knee bends before Jesus and every tongue confesses His lordship. Only the eschaton brings this resolution to the tension, conflict, and animosity that presently define our lives with each other.

8. Verse 13 is explicit and unmistakable in its declaration: "His name alone is exalted." How much room does this leave for the idea that all religions are legitimate expressions of man's spirituality and are to be valued and respected as equally true? What about the idea that other religions simply have "other names" for the same God that we worship? How do we reconcile the need to be socially and culturally sensitive and tolerant with the need to be doctrinally and eternally truthful and faithful?

For many Christians, *this* is the inconvenient truth! Desiring to be good citizens of their republic—which worships tolerance as the ultimate civil virtue and demands that tolerance equal not only recognition but approval of alternate versions of ultimate reality—many Christians struggle mightily with Scripture's insistent and recurrent claim to ultimate and exclusive truth. But the message is clear and incapable of the least compromise: The God of Israel, Yahweh, revealed fully in the person of Jesus of Nazareth, is the only God that is; all other gods, all other interpretations of realty, all other names for God beyond what He has revealed, are false and must be rejected. Names express reality. Wrong names confess a false reality and are therefore wrong. To be able to hold these truths without wavering while extending genuine kindness, compassion, and love for those who do not confess these truths is not some remarkable feat or an inherent contradiction. It is the way that all Christians live—the God they confess, who excludes all pretenders to truth, calls them to such a life . . . to such a love.

9. How does the climax of heavenly praise described in verse 6 differ from the climax of earthly praise related in verse 14? Why is it critical to recognize God's unilateral activity and creation's responsive receptivity as essential to the praise of heaven and earth?

In verse 6, the creatures that dwell in the heavens are reminded of God's glory revealed in the Law with its orderly regularity that defines and animates these heavenly residents. In verse 14, the focus is on what God does for His creatures by lifting up a horn for His people—this is the Gospel, God *doing* for His people. God intervenes with His strong Deliverer and then He brings His people near. There is no better summary of the Gospel, and the perfect fulfillment is evident in the height of the Gospel, the Son incarnate. In both the realm of heaven as well as the region of earth, God is the one who initiates and acts. He establishes the eternal decree, the Law. He lifts up the horn, extending His Gospel. God is God, and we are not. We are not God's peers, His equals, or even His subordinates. We are His creatures. We, the creatures, are the passive and happy recipients of what God accomplishes. Praise is the only possible outcome.

10. *How has this six-week study changed your understanding of what it means to praise God? In light of the truths you have contemplated in this study, what will you do differently?*

Obviously, when answered correctly, this question demands a completely subjective answer. It is to be hoped that even those who claim to have learned nothing will be challenged by the question to consider what they might *do* differently to better express in their own lives the truth explored in this study—the truth they presumably confess.

A Guy's Guide
to Church Lingo

Not everyone can tell a crankshaft from a camshaft, a rooster tail from a red worm, or a divot from a driver. You have to know the lingo (or at least know a mechanic, a bait-and-tackle guy, or a golf pro). Lingo is important, no matter the field, so here are some commonly used Church words and their definitions. Even if you are not already familiar with them, after studying them awhile, you should sound like a pro. Try this: "<u>God</u> has <u>justified</u> me through <u>faith</u> in His Son, <u>Jesus</u> <u>Christ</u>." That wasn't so hard, was it?

–The Editor

Absolve—*to set free from sin*. God absolves us in the Gospel and the Sacraments. Absolution is not merely a symbol. On Christ's behalf, the pastor absolves us after we confess our sins either publicly or privately.

Baptism—*a holy act using water and the Word*. Baptism is not merely a symbol. God truly forgives sins, gives His Holy Spirit, and creates new spiritual life in this Sacrament.

Bible—*God's Word*. There are sixty-six books in the Bible. Because the Holy Spirit inspired each of the Bible's authors to write down every word in the Bible, the Bible is without error.

Christ—*Anointed One* (Greek; in Hebrew: *Messiah*). *Christ* is a title, not Jesus' last name. Jesus is the fulfillment of God's promise to send His Spirit-anointed Son to save us from our sins.

Church—*community of the baptized*. Can also refer to a local congregation or the building in which Christian worship services are held.

Creation—*everything that God our Creator has made*. This includes all planets and stars and satellites, earth, animals, plants, human beings, and spiritual beings we cannot see, such as angels.

Cross—*instrument of torture and death*. By shedding His blood on the cross, Jesus paid the full penalty for our sins and guaranteed that we have God's free and full forgiveness.

Eternal life—*living forever in body and soul in a right relationship with God.* Baptized into Christ, we have God's promise of eternal life, even now in this life.

Faith—*God-given trust in His promises.* Through the Gospel and the Sacraments, God gives us the free gift of faith, which trusts in Jesus alone for salvation.

Forgiveness—*God's act of setting free from the guilt and penalty of sin.* Forgiveness is applied in the Gospel and the Sacraments. Forgiveness is received by all who believe that Jesus is their Savior.

God—*the unseen, almighty, eternal Creator of all that exists.* There is only one God: Father, Son, and Holy Spirit.

Good works—*good deeds.* Ultimately, God performs good works through believers, who are motivated and enabled by His love and forgiveness in Christ. True good works will be rewarded when Jesus returns.

Gospel—*the Good News of forgiveness, life, peace, and joy in Jesus.* The Gospel centers on Jesus' incarnation, life, death, resurrection, ascension, and coming again.

Holy Spirit—*Third Person of the Trinity.* Through God's Word, the Holy Spirit guides, convicts, and comforts us with the truth that our sins are forgiven for the sake of Jesus.

Jesus—*Son of God and Son of Mary.* Jesus lived, died, rose again from the dead, and ascended into heaven for us. One day He will return in glory for us. Jesus is 100 percent God and 100 percent man, although without sin. See *God*.

Justification—*declared in a right relationship with God.* We are justified through faith in Jesus Christ, our God and Savior.

Law—*what God commands or forbids.* The Law restricts outward behavior (curb), confronts us with our sins (mirror), and shows us how to live God's way (guide).

Lord's Supper—*holy act using bread, wine, and the Word.* Also called Holy Communion; the Eucharist. The Lord's Supper is not merely a symbol. Jesus gives us His true body and His true blood in, with, and under the forms of bread and wine to eat and to drink.

Pastor—literally, *"shepherd."* God calls certain men to preach the Gospel and administer the Sacraments in His Church, most usually in a congregation.

Prayer—*communicating with God.* Prayer can be offered alone or with others, out loud or silently, using written prayers, or simply speaking extemporaneously from one's heart. God-pleasing prayers are sincere and are based on God's promises in His Word.

Psalms—*a collection of 150 hymns and poems in the Bible.* Written by David, Solomon, and other writers, many psalms were used in the public worship of Israel. Jesus frequently quoted from the Psalms.

Resurrection—*rising bodily from the dead.* Three days after dying on the cross, Jesus rose from the dead; we now celebrate that day as Easter. When Jesus returns to earth, everyone who has ever lived will be raised from the dead. Those who have trusted in Him will be raised in perfect bodies that will never get sick, grow old, or die.

Sacrament—*holy act instituted by Jesus.* A sacrament is a sacred act instituted by God in which God Himself has joined His Word of promise to a visible element and by which He offers, gives, and seals the forgiveness of sins earned by Christ. By this definition there are two sacraments: Holy Baptism and the Lord's Supper. Sometimes Holy Absolution is counted as a third sacrament, even though it has no divinely instituted visible element.

Salvation—*deliverance.* To be saved means to be delivered from sin, Satan, and death. Jesus is our Savior; He freely gives us His salvation through the Gospel and the Sacraments.

Sanctification—*to be made holy.* After God declares us holy (justification), He makes us holy (sanctification) through the Gospel and the Sacraments so that we begin to do good works in His sight.

Sin—*disobedience to God's Law.* Since Adam and Eve, all humans are born under God's condemnation for the sin that dwells within them, which leads them to commit actual sins. The only way to remove the guilt and penalty of sin is through God's forgiveness.

Son of God—*Second Person of the Trinity.* Jesus is both the Son of God and true man, in one person.

Trinity—"tri-unity," *Three in One.* The Father, the Son, and the Holy Spirit are one God. See *God.*

Word—*God's revelation of Himself.* The Bible is God's Word; Jesus, as the Son of God, is God's Word in human flesh.